HEROES
FOR OUR TIMES

HEROES
FOR OUR TIMES

edited for
The Overseas Press Club of America
**by Will Yolen and
Kenneth Seeman Giniger**

**A GINIGER BOOK
published in association with
STACKPOLE BOOKS**

This book is dedicated to those heroes of the American press, whose names are preserved on the memorial tablet at the Overseas Press Club in New York, who died serving the cause of a free press in a free world.

Contents

Introduction

Who are the heroes of our time? And who are the individuals who should be held up as models, as examples, for our times? Who are the men and women who have left the greatest mark for good upon these times?

These questions prompted the Overseas Press Club of America, an organization of some 3,500 present and former foreign correspondents (with more than 500 members currently stationed overseas for various American media) and others in communications, to poll its membership for their answers.

The results showed Sir Winston Churchill, an honorary member of the Overseas Press Club, as the one individual who has made the greatest mark for good upon our times. Of the 302 different individuals nominated, the "golden dozen," led by Sir Winston, included, in order of the number of votes polled, Franklin D. Roosevelt, John F. Kennedy, Jonas Salk, Mahatma Gandhi, Eleanor Roosevelt, Albert Einstein, Pope John XXIII, Albert Schweitzer, Harry S Truman (also an honorary OPCer), Martin Luther King and Dag Hammarskjöld.

Immediately following these names came those of Adlai Stevenson, Dwight D. Eisenhower, Douglas MacArthur, Helen Keller and George C. Marshall. And the diversity of opinion among OPC members is such that, far down on the list, also appear the names of Josef Stalin, Fidel Castro and Ho Chi Minh, each with one supporter.

This book tells the story of twelve of these heroes for our times. Because many members of the Overseas Press Club, by reason of their work as authors and journalists and photographers, have had the opportunity to know the great figures of our day personally, the Club committee which supervised the preparation of this volume was able to persuade such members as Larry Newman, the Kennedys' next-door neighbor at Hyannis Port; the late Fannie Hurst, a frequent Roosevelt guest at the White House; Dorothy Ducas, closely involved in announcing Jonas Salk's discoveries; and nine other members, all equally distinguished and all with similar firsthand knowledge of their subjects, to write about their heroes.

Men and women professionally engaged in telling the story of our world as they see it encounter many people. Here are the golden dozen they have admired most.

THE EDITORS

1

Winston S. Churchill

By SEYMOUR FREIDIN

SIR WINSTON LEONARD SPENCER CHURCHILL; born Blenheim Palace, Oxfordshire, England, November 30, 1874; son of Lord Randolph Churchill, third son of the 7th Duke of Marlborough, and Jennie Jerome Churchill, born in Brooklyn, New York; educated Harrow and Sandhurst; successively soldier, war correspondent, author, Member of Parliament, Undersecretary for the Colonies, President of the Board of Trade, Home Secretary, First Lord of the Admiralty, Minister of Munitions, Secretary for War and for Air, Colonial Secretary, Chancellor of the Exchequer and Prime Minister; awarded Nobel Prize in Literature, 1953; died London, January 24, 1965.

Seymour Freidin first met Sir Winston during World War II, as a war correspondent in Europe. A reporter for the New York Herald Tribune, *he brought back the first eyewitness account of the battle for Berlin in 1945 and returned to Europe to cover the consolidation of Soviet power in Eastern Europe. He has written articles for most American magazines and was executive editor for foreign news, New York* Herald Tribune. *His book* The Forgotten People *won the 1962 Overseas Press Club annual award for the best book on foreign affairs.*

IT WAS a somber and bitter evening. The Western world was gripped by the melancholia of war in Vietnam. Fresh, explosive onslaughts of Communist forces riddled all thoughts of a faraway, chopped-up country.

In millions of living rooms, watchers and listeners saw hastily processed film of embattled soldiers and agonized people. They heard, in hollow silence, commentaries of explanation. Few, if any, could interpret what it all really meant.

Within a minute, the sound altered. The scene shifted. A voice, gifted with rolling rhetoric, roused those millions from their perplexed torpor. Many knew at once the resonance and the mighty appeal to stamina and greatness. Even the newest generation, coming of age in a combustible world, knew the words.

Across TV screens and through radios poured the voice of Sir Winston Spencer Churchill. It was electrifying to hear the indomitable Englishman who had become the first citizen of the free world, a commoner who dominated a century, a statesman who both made history and wrote it.

And, in a time of crisis like this, the pudgy, round-shouldered aristocrat with the eloquent voice and lion's heart was briefly but appropriately remembered. The troubled times were those he knew and mastered best.

It was the third anniversary of his death and state funeral for which he, himself, wrote the details of the ceremony. When the herald, high in the vaulted dome of St. Paul's Cathedral, blew the dirge of "The Last Post," Churchill became part of history.

But he is inextricably intertwined with contemporary and future history as well as with the past. The wartime

Prime Minister from 1940 to 1945, who rallied Great Britain and a numbed world from the brink of defeat to victory, easily alerts minds and fires imaginations.

A brief remembrance was all it took to roll back the years for his surviving comrades, friends, political colleagues and opposition, the young raised on the Churchillian legend—and the world at large. His enemies were legion. So were his admirers. He was ninety when he died. His name and his monumental achievements have, however, never been interred with him.

Among many newspapermen, I was privileged to have seen him in action in war and peace. When he chose, privately, he could be an awesome talker and thinker aloud. His self-confidence was outsized. He had a right to it. The faint-hearted and the inarticulate Churchill couldn't suffer. Nor could he bear questions about himself.

A little boy was once brought by his mother to Churchill's country place at Chartwell. The boy was promised that he'd meet the greatest man in the world. The little lad slipped away and followed a waiter into Churchill's room.

He marched up to Churchill and asked: "Are you the greatest man in the world?"

"Yes, I am," snarled Sir Winston. "Now push off."

He was, too. Interestingly, quite a few of my friends on the British political scene feel that Churchill's most splendid moments were not during the war but before it. England stood alone in 1940. France had fallen. Nazi Germany was master of most of Europe. Stalin still stood smug, after his deal with Hitler a year earlier.

Through the power of his intellect and the magnetism of his boundless determination, Churchill rallied his nation and much of a shattered world with the great speeches

—"blood, toil, tears and sweat"; "we shall fight in the fields and in the streets, we shall fight in the hills, we shall never surrender"; "this was their finest hour"—that thundered throughout the free world.

Those phrases reverberated across the Atlantic, the length and breadth of the United States. We were still neutral; the Japanese sneak attack on Pearl Harbor came eighteen grim months afterwards.

This was England's greatest ordeal. But Winston Churchill's great ordeal came earlier. With his monumental vision, he thundered unheard, unheeded, virtually unread and unprinted, his great warnings about the growing military power and intentions of Germany. Then, Churchill stood nearly alone against virtually all of England, to say nothing of its allies.

Only thirty months before, Nazi Germany made its monstrous pact with the Soviet Union. Churchill predicted the military tactics of Hitler and his general staff. They were so uncannily accurate that they could be placed unchanged in the history books.

Yet his warnings went unheeded. And his darkest hour came when Anthony Eden (now Lord Avon) resigned on Feb. 20, 1938, as Foreign Secretary against Neville Chamberlain's appeasement of Hitler.

"But on this night of Feb. 20, 1938," he wrote, "and on this occasion alone, sleep deserted me. From midnight till dawn I lay on my bed consumed by emotions of sorrow and fear. I watched the daylight slowly creep in through the windows and saw before me in mental gaze the vision of death."

That was Churchill's darkest hour. Summoned to lead a nation, battered by defeat and stripped of allies, his pessimism fled. He could and did sleep like a baby no matter the trials that beset him. Always refreshed from a sound sleep, he would greet the first stream of officials, propped up in bed, chewing a huge cigar. Remember, he became Prime Minister at the age of sixty-five, when most men retire.

The darkest hour for England came shortly after he took up the post of Prime Minister. It was Sept. 15, 1940. Churchill inquired of an immediate subordinate, an old acquaintance of mine: "How many Spitfires have we in reserve?"

"None, sir," was my friend's chilling reply.

"Then we must press forward the attack," said Churchill lightheartedly. That was the night the German air armadas finally desisted.

The Battle of Britain was over. Churchill was the beloved indomitable hero of the whole free world. There remain many, including a close and valued friend high in the present Labour government, who liked him best when he was unloved—and still indomitable.

"That's the true best," remarked that Minister recently, utterly reverential of all of Churchill's wartime feats.

Churchill possessed to his finger tips that indefinable talent and quality called "style." Yet hailed as he was for his herculean efforts during the war, the British electorate turned on him in mid-1945. They deposed Churchill and his Conservatives from office as he stood in his fullest glory.

Magnificent as he had been as war chief, Churchill was seen as an imperialist and advocate of the old order by the voters. They preferred a Labour regime to grapple with postwar problems at home, with delicate settlements abroad. The late Clement Attlee became Prime Minister.

Shortly after the returns were in, I asked Churchill (he was not knighted until 1953) how he saw his political future. He stared down at the drinks on the table and flicked a dead cigar. When he looked up, his reply was succinct: "I shall try, as long as my powers are with me, to become Prime Minister."

In loyal opposition, he waited six years. During that long interval, he warned the world about the ruthlessness of Stalin and his Soviet empire. It was at Fulton, Missouri, that he made another famous speech, warning of the "Iron Curtain."

Churchill loved the United States in general and Americans in particular. He was half American, his mother having been the former Jennie Jerome, a Brooklyn-born beauty, daughter of a wealthy American. Between the two world wars and afterwards, he visited the States frequently.

In the spring of 1963, Churchill was greatly touched by an unprecedented honor. The American Congress voted him an honorary citizen of the U.S. As proof, he was given a handsome, specially designed U.S. passport.

It was a balmy day—for London, that is—July 28, 1964, when Churchill visited the House of Commons for the last time. The Mother of Parliaments, ancient citadel of parliamentary democracy, was packed and hushed. In black coat and striped trousers, polka-dot bowtie in place, the great, old man sat mute as the House cheered. When he departed, tread hesitant, he was hailed by every onlooker. As he slowly left the House—"I am a child of the House of Commons," he so often liked to say—cheers split the air again.

With the ghost of a smile, Sir Winston raised his right hand and showed the two fingers of the V-for-Victory sign Britain came to know so endearingly during World War II. It was the last time he saw the House of Commons but he left an imprint no other member ever managed.

The day after, former Prime Minister Harold Macmillan, then seventy, rose and summed Sir Winston up in thirty-five words:

"The oldest among us can recall nothing to compare with him and the younger ones among you will never see the like again. He was the greatest Member of Parliament of this or any age."

For the last two years of his parliamentary life, Sir John Langford-Holt was assigned, by silent agreement, to see to it that Churchill had help if needed when he came to the Commons. Langford-Holt, a Tory (vernacular for Conservative) MP, remembers so vividly how Churchill on these visits motioned to people to leave him alone. Sir Winston would grip his cane and totter down the gangway.

Langford-Holt walked with him. All of the Commons looked away. There wasn't a member, no matter his political feelings, who could bear to see if Churchill ever fell down in their presence.

"I hated it," remembers Langford-Holt. "There we were, insignificant people who never led or could hope to lead his life. We were being patronizing to him. It simply was not right. This is no eulogy to the man. He had all the flaws of a human being; he was wrong many times. He was obstinate and temperish. But he was great and we are insignificant and I felt wrong."

When many veteran members of today's House of Commons weren't even born, Churchill was a senior minister in a pre–World War I Cabinet. He had already made his mark as a soldier, war correspondent, journalist and writer. By the time he was first appointed a Cabinet minister, Churchill had been in battle many times in far-flung parts of the world—Cuba, India, South Africa and the Sudan.

At twenty-four, on Sept. 2, 1898, at Omdurman in the Sudan, he rode in the famous charge of the 21st Lancers. That gallant, if foolhardy, maneuver has been depicted in many movies, 300 men charging at 3,000 kneeling riflemen. Churchill used a pistol and emerged unscathed.

Gunfire never fazed him. As a World War I minister, he was restless as always. When the Dardanelles disaster in Turkey was blamed on him, Churchill sought and was assigned to trench warfare in France. He was forty at the time.

An aged, surviving comrade of the 6th Royal Scots Fusiliers recalls Sir Winston this way: "He was indifferent to shellfire. Only a major then, he rebuked generals. They never knew or dared to challenge him. Winston was impatient. He wanted to win."

After a tingling spell in trench warfare, Churchill was recalled to civilian life, again to the Cabinet as Minister of Munitions. He went from one taxing assignment to another, high in government, as the war ended and in the aftermath.

As a man, Sir Winston was every bit as interesting a study as Sir Winston, the international personality. Son of Lord Randolph Churchill, Sir Winston was reared in fine circumstances and knew quality.

"Winston is easy to please," a friend said. "All he wants is the best of everything."

He himself often remarked on his enjoyment of Scotch whisky and French brandy. Impishly, he also frequently furthered the rumor that he used these in great quantities. But his long-time bodyguard, Walter H. Thompson, scotched most of those tales.

He said that actually Sir Winston drank moderately and that he chewed cigars more than he smoked them.

Thompson recalled vividly Churchill's rich vocabulary for cursing. There were spates of "vile temper," habitual impatience and the attitude of a "bullying schoolmaster."

When he was happy, Thompson remembered, Sir Winston hummed loudly and tunelessly. He "sounded like a mass of insects." On occasions when he tried to drive a car, Churchill sought to bully his way through traffic. And one of his famous brick walls—Churchill adored bricklaying as well as painting for relaxation—had to be torn down while he was at lunch. The wall was hastily rebuilt lest a "puff of wind," as Thompson remembered, blow it over.

By the time of his eighty-second birthday, Sir Winston was somewhat enfeebled. But, on that occasion, a photographer called out that he hoped to take his picture on his one hundredth birthday. Sir Winston eyed him and replied: "I see no reason why you shouldn't, young man. You look hale and hearty enough."

In his enormously rich lifetime, Sir Winston encountered nearly every major personality who influenced the world in assorted epochs. They included Queen Victoria, Prime Ministers Arthur James Balfour and David Lloyd George, Premier Georges Clemenceau, Kaiser Wilhelm, Presidents Theodore Roosevelt and Woodrow Wilson, General John J. Pershing, Marshal Ferdinand Foch and his own World War I commanders such as Field Marshal Earl Haig.

These are only random names, out of a huge list. Subsequently there were Presidents Franklin D. Roosevelt, Harry S Truman and Dwight D. Eisenhower, whom Sir Winston first knew as Allied Supreme Commander. Add to that roster Soviet dictator and wartime ally Stalin; exile leaders including Czechoslovakia's President Eduard Beneš; and, of course, Gen. Charles de Gaulle, whom

Churchill helped rescue from overrun France and supported under the most trying circumstances.

The Free French insignia under De Gaulle was the Cross of Lorraine. After a particularly difficult session with De Gaulle, Churchill remarked to associates with a sigh, "The most burdensome cross I have to bear is the Cross of Lorraine."

Sir Winston's output as author alone might have been a whole career for any other highly talented man. He wrote more than thirty books. His most impressive work was a six-volume history of World War II. The titles had a Churchillian ring—*The Gathering Storm, The Finest Hour, The Grand Alliance, The Hinge of Fate, Closing the Ring,* and *Triumph and Tragedy.*

The last of these came out on his 79th birthday. It bore the ironic superscription, "How the great democracies triumphed and so were able to resume the follies which had so nearly cost them their life."

For the war history, and also for his stirring wartime speeches, Sir Winston received the 1953 Nobel Prize in literature. By then, he already was at work on another series, "A History of the English-Speaking Peoples." It was a study he had started before the war.

Until 1953, Sir Winston all his life had cherished his status as simply Mr. Winston Churchill. Let others wear the titles, he said. At seventy-nine, after a life of service, he relented. On April 25, 1953, he knelt in Windsor Castle before Queen Elizabeth II, felt a sword tap on each shoulder and arose as Sir Winston. He had become a member of the oldest and most exclusive order of knighthood—"The Most Noble Order of the Garter."

Sir Winston was exceedingly fond of his handsome Queen. He was her honorary uncle. Churchill first saw the child Britain hoped would usher in a new Elizabethan age when she ascended the throne as an infant in a crib.

Sir Winston often counseled her in matters both private and state. In January 1957, when illness forced Sir Anthony Eden out as Prime Minister, Sir Winston was one of the few consulted by the Queen in selecting Harold Macmillan as successor.

Two years before, on his own initiative, Sir Winston had resigned the No. 1 political post, on April 5, 1955. Spring general elections were at hand. He had suffered strokes in 1950 and 1953. The second one paralyzed him completely for a time. Having made up his mind, he drove to Buckingham Palace. There he tendered his resignation to Queen Elizabeth II. It was a moving and dramatic moment. Churchill recalled that another Queen—Victoria, the present monarch's great-great-grandmother—sat on the throne when he began his public life so long before.

A far fresher recollection was of the previous night. At a farewell dinner, he had proposed the traditional toast to the Queen. In a gesture never before offered by a British monarch, she then arose and responded with a toast "to my Prime Minister."

His resignation marked the end of an epoch. Virtually all of his contemporaries were gone, notably Roosevelt and Stalin, with whom he had worked so closely during World War II. Britain and the world would still hear from him as elder statesman and back-bencher in Commons. He resigned only his office, not his seat in the House of Commons. And, as an indefatigable author, he would still publish several books. But he was through as principal actor at front and center of the stage.

Sir Winston gave two reasons for resigning. The first was age. The second was that he wanted to give his successor,

Sir Anthony Eden, the opportunity of putting his program before the country in the coming elections.

Friends said there was one more element in the picture. It was that Lady Churchill—the former Miss Clementine Hozier, whom he married in 1908—had persuaded him to give his remaining years to her.

Of his own personal life Sir Winston confined himself to the comment, "I was married and lived happily ever afterward."

After about fifteen years of married life, Mrs. Churchill told a friend that she thought, in case anything sudden happened to her, she had better leave behind instructions: "How to Manage Winston Churchill."

They had four daughters, of whom two survive, and a son, Randolph. A grandson, named for his formidable grandfather, Winston, only 27, is already retracing the great man's steps: war correspondent, writer, politician. His son, Sir Winston's great-grandson, was born just before Churchill died.

In resigning as Prime Minister, Sir Winston turned down an offer of a dukedom, just as he had refused an offer of an earldom after World War II. He told Queen Elizabeth he wanted to continue as a House of Commons man.

And continue he did. In the general elections of 1959, he defeated his Labour opponent. Two weeks later, when he took his oath of office, both sides in the House of Commons cheered.

But the old indestructible battler—victor over so many bouts with illness, injury and crisis—was beginning to slow down. In 1960, in a bedroom fall, he broke a small bone in his back. Two years later, in a fall at Monte Carlo, he broke his left thigh bone.

Recovery was slow. On May 14, 1963, he visited Commons for the first time in nearly a year. Meantime, he announced that he would not run again in 1964.

Sir Winston had always driven himself hard. He had almost an animal love of the night. This wearied secretaries who had to sit up for his late working sessions. He had, however, his own health rules and followed them closely. Every day he took a long afternoon nap. For relaxation, he also had one or two hot baths daily.

His complete recovery from several bouts with pneumonia and some major surgery in 1947 showed his good physical condition.

It was on Nov. 30, 1874, that the future great man was born at Blenheim Palace, Woodstock, Oxfordshire, ancestral seat of the Dukes of Marlborough. Lord Randolph Churchill, father of the redhaired baby and third son of the 7th Duke of Marlborough, was a meteor who flamed briefly in British politics. He quarreled with the then Prime Minister, Lord Salisbury, and walked out. Churchill's father died young, at forty-four.

In mentioning his parents, British father and American mother, Churchill told the U.S. Congress in Washington soon after Pearl Harbor: "I cannot help reflecting that if my father had been American and my mother British . . . I might have got here on my own."

He stood five feet, eight inches tall, and had twinkling blue eyes and a stubborn jaw. In World War II, his visage was often caricatured as a bulldog's. He was, however, so cherubic in mien that he could say, "All babies look like me." He walked with a slight forward stoop and was almost never without a cigar.

As a boy, he grew up in pleasant days of plenty. He had a thousand lead soldiers to deploy in battle line on the nursery floor. He had a donkey to ride and, later, horses.

The young Churchill loved history and poetry and "Punch" cartoons. He detested the classics.

Often he was stubborn and strong-willed. But his mind was tremendously active. A dancing teacher found young Churchill "the naughtiest boy in the class" and "possibly the naughtiest boy in the world."

After nearly failing at Harrow, one of Britain's famed and ancient public schools, he went on to Sandhurst, the West Point of Britain. In 1895, he was graduated at twenty with a commission as subaltern in the 4th (Queen's Own) Hussars. By then, his mastery of the English language was well developed.

Churchill once explained his accomplishment. At Harrow, as a boy, he stayed in the lowest form thrice too long, studying English while others went on to Latin and Greek. "Thus, I got into my bones," he said, "the essential structure of the ordinary English sentence—which is a noble thing."

But his love for action was also fierce. As a young hussar, he wanted to fight and right away. Through a family friend, the British Ambassador at Madrid, he promoted a leave. He got an assignment to go to Cuba to watch the Spaniards fight local guerrillas. In Cuba, he marched through thick jungles with Spanish forces, heard stray rifle shots, saw that the noise exceeded casualties. He also learned to love cigars. For this assignment, Churchill acquired the Spanish Military Order of Merit to decorate his chest.

Back in London, he wined, dined and played polo. Then he went with his regiment to India at the height of British imperial rule. He played more polo and discovered he was sadly under-educated. He began to devour history, philosophy, poetry, Plato, Darwin, Schopenhauer and a fat book of quotations.

In 1897, fighting started on India's northwest border. Churchill's regiment was not involved. Overnight, he got a leave and a war correspondent's job with an Indian newspaper and the London *Daily Telegraph*. At the front with the Malakand Field Force, he found real Kipling stuff. War correspondents, especially Winston Churchill, were not held to a spectator's role.

He shot down several tribesmen and won another medal. But his leave expired. He was sent back to play polo with the Hussars. Finding that his news stories had been well received in London, he immediately wrote a book, *The Story of the Malakand Field Force*. It won high praise.

Bright with success, he next tried his first and only novel, *Savrola, a Tale of the Revolution in Laurania*. It earned him £700, a handsome sum in those days. Yet Churchill always advised his friends not to read it.

In 1898, Sir Herbert Kitchener, later Lord Kitchener, was preparing to wipe out the Mahdists in the Anglo-Egyptian Sudan. Subaltern Churchill applied to Kitchener for service. He was refused. Kitchener didn't like the way the young soldier-writer criticized superiors.

Finally, with his mother's help through a family friend at the War Office, Sir Winston got assigned to the Egyptian force. It was without pay and at his own expense. In other words, he paid for the privilege of risking death in Egypt.

After his exploits in the famed cavalry charge at Omdurman, Churchill returned to London. He wrote another book, of course, which criticized Kitchener. Churchill now decided to be a writer. First, he went back to India where he discharged his duty with the Hussars by helping them win a polo tournament. Then he resigned and came home a civilian.

He already had a known name through his writing. In 1899, the Conservatives of Oldham asked him to run for Commons when their candidate died. He agreed and was defeated. But he didn't care because the Boer War was starting and he was off to cover it for the *Morning Post.*

Churchill returned from the war in South Africa quite a figure—the hero of a sensational escape after capture by the Boers. The Conservatives, with an election on their hands in 1900, asked him again to contest the Commons seat for Oldham. This he won, and a fantastic political career began.

Members of Parliament were unpaid in 1900. Before settling into the hurly-burly of politics, Sir Winston wrote two more books to make money. He also made a long lecture tour, even to the U.S. and Canada. His audiences were roused by the hair-raising tale of his escape from the Boers.

Churchill's fluency with pen and word was eventually to earn him a munificent and steady income. He usually collected an annual figure upwards of $100,000. It's big money today, but it was enormous in those days.

Whether writing, speaking or politicking, Sir Winston had an independent streak that defied party discipline. In 1904, his uncompromising independence finally broke the party lines. The Conservatives revived the protective tariff. Sir Winston, as a free-trader, lit into them. One night, when he rose to speak, all the Conservatives walked out. He responded by joining the Liberals.

It was a good move. The Liberals won in 1905 and named him Under-Secretary for the Colonies. He was then thirty-one. Three years later, when Herbert Asquith became Prime Minister, Churchill was elevated to the Cabinet as President of the Board of Trade. The same year that he was initiated into Cabinet government at 10 Downing Street—which he came to know so well—he married Miss Hozier.

He kept climbing. In 1910, Sir Winston was raised to Home Secretary. Yet fellow Cabinet members worried about him. Lord Haldane observed: "He is too apt to act first and think afterward—though of his energy and courage one cannot speak too highly."

Within a year, Churchill was named First Lord of the Admiralty. This was a most important job. For several years the Germans had been trying to rival Britain's naval power. If war came, Britain would stand or fall on her naval strength and, at thirty-seven, Churchill was responsible for it.

Characteristically, he began to fire old admirals, converted ships from coal to oil and bought into the Iranian oil fields as a source of supply. He raised sailors' pay and pushed submarine development. A year before World War I, Churchill learned to fly in a creaky biplane over Southampton. Shortly before the war exploded, his naval review sported a hundred planes, some of which could actually launch torpedoes.

The British naval review in the fateful summer of 1914 ended on July 20, three days before the assassination of the heir to the throne of Austria-Hungary resulted in Austria's ultimatum to Serbia. Normally, the British fleet would have been split up and the reserves sent back home. But Churchill, acting on his own, kept the fleet mobilized. It was ready and waiting in the North Sea when war broke out a few days later.

Sir Winston was always daring in war, but within a year,

his daring put him in the doghouse. Sensing futility in the land deadlock on the Western front, he decided he could shorten the war by taking Constantinople from the Turks. This would open the Black Sea for Allied communication with Russia.

Historians still argue about the Dardanelles campaign. It failed and cost the Allies more than 200,000 killed and wounded. It also cost Sir Winston his job. The heckling cry of "Gallipoli" from political audiences haunted him long afterward.

Off he went, then, to France and trench warfare. By mid-1916, he was a civilian again. A few months later, through his friendship with David Lloyd George, by this time Prime Minister, the resilient Sir Winston bounced back into the Cabinet as Minister of Munitions. After the war ended, he was appointed War and Air Secretary, then Colonial Secretary.

Later in 1922, the coalition government left over from the war ceased to exist. In the resulting election, Churchill was emphatically rejected for a seat in Commons by the voters at Dundee. They elected a Prohibitionist named Scrymgeour.

Determinedly, Churchill persisted in his quest for a seat in Parliament. In two successive years, 1923 and 1924, he was beaten. But the vagaries of British politics were as unpredictable as Sir Winston's tenacity was strong.

Late in 1924, the long-exiled Conservatives were preparing to take over the government again. It developed that they wanted Churchill back. He had pleased them with his anti-Bolshevist stand. Without ceremony, he stepped quietly back into the Conservative fold he abandoned twenty years earlier. He was elected to Commons.

To the surprise of all England, Prime Minister Stanley

Baldwin named him Chancellor of the Exchequer, which is like being a super-Secretary of the U.S. Treasury. Sir Winston was sentimental about this. It was his father's old Cabinet post. He did a good job until the Baldwin government fell in 1929.

Sir Winston once again withdrew to the back benches. He was still the most eloquent and most prolific speaker in the House. But he was no longer considered a potential Prime Minister. Churchill was getting along in years; he was fifty-five.

When Hitler took over Germany in 1933, Sir Winston recognized the man immediately as evil incarnate. He begged for more airplanes, warning: "This cursed, hellish invention and development of war from the air has revolutionized our position. We are not the same kind of country we used to be when we were an island, only twenty-five years ago."

Britons could well remember those words a few years later when the Luftwaffe was blasting their land. This was the start of the great career that made Sir Winston the most popular man in England when the Second World War began. At first, people scoffed at him. Then they believed him. And finally they hailed him as the one man who knew all along what would happen.

Disarmament conferences failed. The League of Nations fell apart. The world headed for war. Sir Winston roared on against Baldwin, Ramsay MacDonald and Neville Chamberlain for leaving England weak. He was bitter over Chamberlain's appeasement policy, as sadly symbolized by the sacrifice of Czechoslovakia at Munich. Moreover, he grew so aware of the Nazi danger that he even demanded an alliance with Communist Russia, a country for which he had little respect.

After swallowing up the Rhineland, Austria and Czechoslovakia, Hitler pounced on Poland. His way lay clear because of a cynical power arrangement with Stalin in the late summer of 1939. Britain declared war on Germany on Sept. 3. On that day, Sir Winston returned to the Cabinet in his old post as First Lord of the Admiralty.

A man of war from his youth, Sir Winston was the moving spirit of the war Cabinet from the start. Repeated shuffles gave him more and more authority. Finally, after Britain's weak and unsuccessful expedition to oppose the Germans in Norway, Chamberlain could hold out no longer. Winston Churchill became Prime Minister and Minister of Defense and fought the war to the end in his own way.

Churchill had a rich and varied preparation when he first became Prime Minister at sixty-five. There had been his careers as a soldier, writer and stormy petrel of politics. He had been brilliant and difficult in them all. A memorable assessment of one of his books came from Lord Balfour. He described Churchill's World War I history as, "Winston Churchill's brilliant autobiography, disguised as a history of the universe."

But, on one thing, Churchill's record was clear and persistent. From the moment that Adolf Hitler achieved major status in German politics, Churchill recognized him as a menace to Britain and the world. Year in and year out, from 1933 on, he warned his country about the Nazis. Writing of the Hitlerian menace in 1936, he urged: "Stop it! Stop it! Stop it now!"

So, when nine months of World War II led to the direst disaster, Sir Winston was called to head the government. It was May 10, 1940. The fall of France and Dunkirk were just weeks ahead. Britain stood alone and the Germans were building invasion barges across the English Channel.

Churchill didn't try to fool anybody. "Hitler knows that he will have to break us in this island or lose the war," he told the Britons. "If we can stand up to him, all Europe may be free."

A bit later, when bomb-battered Britain cried out for revenge raids against Germany, Churchill replied, "Business before pleasure." His few bombers were needed for military targets.

And so, under Sir Winston, Britain fought and won the Battle of Britain in the air. Hitler, who might have invaded Britain when it was woefully weak, dallied, hesitated and finally missed the bus.

Radio audiences came to know Churchill's golden words. He was a great speaker, though with quiet, almost throaty delivery. There was a slight difficulty for him in handling the letter "s." It was all that remained of a youthful lisp. His words carried not only information but a sense of glory and grand deeds. His voice dripped scorn when he called Hitler a "bloody guttersnipe" and went hard on the letter "z" when he spoke contemptuously of Nazis.

Mussolini, he demolished as a "tattered lackey." Italian Fascists he rarely even deigned to mention, so profound was his contempt for them.

When the U.S. declared war, Sir Winston said candidly, "This is what I have dreamed of, aimed at and worked for, and now it has come to pass."

Sir Winston and President Roosevelt were good friends and close workers—as were other presidents of his time, Truman and Eisenhower. He never met Kennedy. His wartime association with Roosevelt was especially close. They were both Navy buffs and both of wealthy background.

Action, always action, was something Sir Winston loved. General Eisenhower flatly refused to let him go into Normandy on D-Day with the invasion troops. But a few months later, in March, 1945, he crossed the Rhine River atop an amphibious vehicle. He was completely in character, crying out, "On we go . . . we are driving back a beaten army."

It was on a bridge over the Rhine that some of us, hotfooting it down from an American sector, joined Churchill. His commander, Field Marshal Bernard L. Montgomery (now Viscount Montgomery of Alamein), was escorting the Prime Minister. Suddenly, Churchill paused. He leaned over the bridge and relieved himself on the murky waters below. Everyone followed suit as Churchill growled, "I've been waiting a long time for that."

There had been great adversities and setbacks from the time he became Prime Minister to the Rhine. The die was cast, though, when Russia and the U.S. entered hostilities. And Sir Winston became the most venturesome of all the allied war leaders.

He had flown to Europe just before France collapsed and made a last-ditch offer of union with Britain. The next year saw the meeting at sea with Roosevelt and the birth of the Atlantic Charter. He made four wartime trips to Washington. He visited Quebec twice, Moscow twice, the North African battlefronts, Malta, Egypt, Greece, Italy and defeated Germany. Then there were the official conferences of the Allied Powers at Cairo, Teheran, Casablanca, Yalta and Potsdam.

Sir Winston was at the Potsdam conference in 1945 when the British turned him out of office. It was strange.

He was personally popular almost beyond belief. But his party was not trusted with the postwar problems just ahead.

Back to London went Churchill, where he drove to Buckingham Palace, resigned, moved out of 10 Downing Street and went house-hunting. Though out of leadership, Sir Winston was re-elected as M.P. from Woodford, Essex, and as opposition chief. He constantly assailed the government of Labour Prime Minister Attlee. The socialization policies of Labour were repugnant to him. And he was almost sick at heart to see units of the Empire, one by one, become independent.

Soon he was attacking the Soviet Union, communism and Stalin as threats to civilization and peace. Stalin denounced him as a "warmonger." In Fulton, Missouri, on March 5, 1946, came the "Iron Curtain" speech.

From Stettin in the Baltic to Trieste in the Adriatic," he declared, "an Iron Curtain has descended across the continent."

It was on Oct. 26, 1951, that Sir Winston was called back to be Prime Minister. Economic difficulties loomed large—adverse dollar gap, devaluated pound, loss of oil assets in Iran and investments in Red China, stiffening competition in world markets and staggering costs of arms.

The strain of great responsibility and age began to take its toll of the man who towered above the rest of the world. He was eighty when he resigned. His energies were now truncated. He was a fair painter of natural scenes, with a flair for bright colors. Even painting became burdensome. Yet he managed, before he died, to write out the lines his funeral should follow.

The world kept a death watch as life ebbed painlessly from Sir Winston at his town house at 28 Hyde Park Gate. But the medical world marveled how the ninety-year-old statesman fought for ten days. He died in his sleep at 8:05 A.M. Jan. 24, 1965, and immediately flags were lowered and church bells tolled. Britain was plunged in mourning for her greatest son.

At the behest of Queen Elizabeth, Churchill lay in state for three days. He reposed on a great catafalque in the ancient chamber of Westminster Hall at the House of Commons. In biting cold, great queues waited patiently their turn to enter and pay homage. There were the elderly down to youngsters and babes in arms who filed solemnly past the catafalque.

Great names of contemporary history appeared. Old enmities were forgotten. General de Gaulle, in uniform, stood in silent salute at Westminster Hall. On a gray Saturday, January 30, all London turned out for the last farewell to Sir Winston. Every branch of military service was represented. A caisson hauled the coffin, atop which had been placed many of Sir Winston's orders and decorations.

At the architectural gem that is St. Paul's Cathedral, a service and prayers were intoned for Sir Winston. Then, he was borne on a barge across the Thames to a waiting train. He was buried in the ancient cemetery at Bladon, a mile from Blenheim Palace where he was born.

At every anniversary of Sir Winston's death, wreaths are placed high on his grave. One always stands out. It reads, "To my darling Winston—Clemmie," from his wife. All Britain and most of the world share her feelings and her loss. Churchill was our last great monument.

2

Franklin D. Roosevelt

By ALDEN HATCH

FRANKLIN DELANO ROOSEVELT; born Hyde Park, New York, Jan. 30, 1882; son of James Roosevelt and Sara Delano Roosevelt; educated Groton, Harvard and Columbia Law School; lawyer, New York State Senator, Assistant Secretary of the Navy, vice presidential nominee, governor of New York, and four times President (32d) of the United States succeeding Herbert Hoover; paralyzed by poliomyelitis in 1921, he eventually recovered partial use of his legs but remained crippled for the rest of his life; died Warm Springs, Georgia, April 12, 1945; died in office, succeeded as president by Harry S Truman.

Alden Hatch, one of America's most prolific biographers of contemporary figures, has been a friend of the Roosevelt family for many years and spends half his time in the Hudson River valley where FDR was born. He has written biographies of three presidents of the United States, including Roosevelt, and three popes among his thirty-two published books. His work is known throughout the world and has been translated into ten languages. He feels particularly close to Franklin Roosevelt because his own success has involved conquest of the obstacle of a crippling disease in childhood.

FRANKLIN DELANO ROOSEVELT was one of the great presidents of the United States. Of course, it was not all inherent greatness. It was also timing and luck. Yet the cards were stacked against Franklin Roosevelt—or seemed to be. He was well-born when presidents were still supposed to be born in log cabins. He was rich when the fashion was for politicians to be poor. He was a mama's boy—what a mama he had! And he could not even walk.

Up there in the Hudson River Valley, Franklin Roosevelt and his friends lived in a closed society. Even in 1880, when Roosevelt was born, the Valley was a little decadent. The great years, the years of the patroons who held their big manors by royal grant were spent. So were the people. Chancellor Robert Livingston, who helped to write the Declaration of Independence, but did not bother to sign it, and negotiated the Louisiana Purchase; Gouverneur Morris; the Phillipses, Van Burens, Jays, Van Rensselaers, Stuyvesants, and Delanos—all had been succeeded on their diminishing estates by descendants who lacked the drive of these history-makers. It was becoming the matriarchy the Valley remains today because the women were stronger than their men.

Roosevelt's mother Sara Delano was strong. She fell in love with James Roosevelt, who was a widower over fifty, and married him. They had one child—Franklin—their darling, their hope, their justification for living. It has been said that Franklin Roosevelt climbed the ladder of success one step at a time—he started out in a private car and ended up in a special train. But that sort of beginning makes it harder to be great.

Young Roosevelt had remarkable gifts, not just the

money and his aristocratic birth; he was intelligent, witty, genial, a good athlete and very beautiful. That adjective is not supposed to be used about a man; one should say handsome, attractive, stunning. But why mince around? Roosevelt was as beautiful as an eight-point stag standing on a hilltop in the sunset. And as male. He also had a superb speaking voice. The trouble he had was that it was all too easy.

Roosevelt met his first president at the age of seven. His father took him to call on Grover Cleveland. In those days a man like James Roosevelt could just drop in on the President. Cleveland was rather taken with the handsome little boy. He gave him a sound piece of advice. "Whatever you do, Franklin," he said, "don't ever become President of the United States."

In his youth, Franklin Roosevelt followed the pattern of his kind. He went to Groton, the most fashionable prep school of all and one of the best. Then to Harvard. He made good grades and the best clubs. In 1900, when he was a freshman, his father died, and the matriarchy began. Sara Delano had been deeply in love with her husband. Now Franklin was all she had left and she meant to keep him. She did not quite succeed.

Against all probability, Franklin fell in love with his distant cousin, Eleanor Roosevelt. She was regarded as the ugly duckling of the whole Roosevelt clan, a shy introvert terribly conscious of her awkwardness. She was very sweet and gratefully unbelieving that so brilliant a creature as her cousin Franklin could possibly care for her. Of course, underneath that simple exterior there was a brain almost as good as his. But it did not show.

Sara did her best to break it up. She tempted Franklin with all the kingdoms of this world. But he had made up his mind; they were married in 1905. It was a magnificent wedding. President Theodore Roosevelt gave his niece away and stole the show. After standing in the receiving line for a few minutes, he moved into the dining room. The whole crowd—guests, bridesmaids, ushers—followed the dynamic president. The bride and groom were left standing alone. Franklin smiled at Eleanor and said, "Well, we may as well join the party."

The young Roosevelts did not have to worry about money. Between them they had $10,000 a year, and the older Mrs. Roosevelt was worth a million or more. In 1907, she built two handsome town houses for herself and her son at 45–47 East 65th Street in Manhattan. They had a single entrance lobby and a connecting door on the second floor. She intended to keep the umbilical cord intact. Eleanor did not like it, but she was busy having children.

Franklin attended Columbia Law School, but, when he passed the New York State Bar examinations, he left without bothering to graduate. He got a job with the illustrious law firm of Carter, Ledyard and Milburn. Whatever they paid him, he was not worth it.

Roosevelt was a poor lawyer, not from lack of ability but because the law bored him. He did not have the self-discipline to do things he did not like. The things that interested him he did superbly well. These were anything connected with the sea, from sailing small boats to naval history; international relations; and politics, especially politics.

Franklin got his first chance at his favorite avocation in 1910. Hyde Park, just north of Poughkeepsie, was the Roosevelts' home. That summer the Democratic Party chiefs were looking for a candidate foolish enough to run for the New York State Senate from that hopelessly Republican district. They offered the nomination to young Roosevelt, who accepted. He put on a brilliant campaign and, to the amazement of those old pros, he won. That same year Democrat John A. Dix was elected Governor of New York and Woodrow Wilson, Governor of New Jersey.

In his first term as State Senator, Roosevelt broke with the party bosses to lead a group of liberal young Democrats in blocking the election of a party hack, William ("Blue-Eyed Billy") Sheehan, as United States Senator in favor of State Supreme Court Justice James O'Gorman. This gained him nationwide attention. But, even more important to his career, he established a close friendship with the Albany correspondent of the New York *Herald,* a little, gnome-like man named Louis McHenry Howe.

In 1912, a flood tide of liberalism was running against the stand-pat Republicanism of President William Howard Taft. Its leader was Governor Woodrow Wilson of New Jersey, who voiced the idealistic aspirations of progress-minded Democrats. Roosevelt admired him tremendously and, in the hard-fought Democratic National Convention of 1912, he was helpful in securing the presidential nomination for Wilson. When Wilson was elected president that November, he offered Franklin Roosevelt the job he wanted most, Assistant Secretary of the Navy.

Secretary of the Navy Josephus Daniels was a courteous gentleman and a first-rate politician, who did not know a ship's bow from her stern. Roosevelt liked him and they made a fine team, dividing the work according to their talents. Daniels concentrated on the president and Congress; Roosevelt handled the admirals, who disliked the Secretary, and managed the technical details of running one of the greatest navies in the world. The responsibility might have crushed a man only thirty-one years old; it buoyed Franklin up.

He brought Louis Howe with him as his assistant. They found the Navy was as full of deadwood as a Spanish galleon's stern. The fat years of peace and the rule of seniority had filled the high command with the naval equivalent of Colonel Blimps; the morale of the sailors was low. Roosevelt devoted his tremendous energy and love of the service to modernizing it. By the time the United States entered World War I in April, 1917, it was fighting fit and ready to go.

Never did America enter a war more unitedly or more idealistically. Roosevelt, like his kinsman Theodore, had been for it ever since a German submarine had sunk the *Lusitania* two years before. Now he was unleashed. His previous spurts of energy were insignificant compared to the activity he now showed. Since Daniels still knew comparatively little about ships and the sea, Roosevelt, for all practical purposes, ran the whole show. He turned down an offer to run for Governor of New York to stay on the job and suggested Alfred E. Smith instead.

In rapid succession Roosevelt organized the Eyes of the Navy to borrow binoculars for the rapidly expanding fleet; created the Macy Board to assure adequate labor for the humming navy yards; invented the small motor-powered sub-chaser, with his friend Loring S. Wasey, to combat the deadly U-boats; and forced through the decision to lay a 240-mile chain of mines in the North Sea to pen the U-boats in their German bases. He pushed forward the regular operations with extraordinary speed. The splendid record of the United States Navy in World War I was due as much to him as to any other single person.

Then came the peace that turned out to be only a long armistice. Roosevelt watched with dismay Wilson's mishandling of the Senate that led to its rejection of the Treaty of Versailles and the League of Nations in which he ardently believed. "If I were doing it," he said to Eleanor, "I'd take the Senate, and maybe the House, into my confidence, get them committed to it and work out the details later."

The Democratic National Convention of 1920 nominated Governor James M. Cox of Ohio for president. They needed a man from a big eastern state to balance the ticket. To his real amazement, Franklin Roosevelt heard himself nominated for vice-president by acclamation. Of course, Cox and Roosevelt never had a chance, campaigning for the League of Nations. President Wilson was ill and discredited by the failure of the Senate to ratify the Treaty of Versailles. The country was tired of idealism and foreign adventures. Republican candidate Warren Gamaliel Harding struck exactly the right note when he called for a return to "normalcy." He was elected by an overwhelming majority. Though he lost, Franklin Roosevelt, campaigning all across the land, impressed his charming image on the minds of the voters. He was directly in line for greater things.

In the summer of 1921, the Roosevelts were all together at Campobello Island for the first time since the War. There were seven of them now, Franklin and Eleanor, Anna, James, Elliott, Franklin, Jr., and John. It was a happy time until. . . .

The story of paralysis striking in the night; the agonizing days of fever and despair; Roosevelt's incredible courage as he faced death or, at best, hopeless invalidism; and Eleanor's gallant support of her husband, has often been told. When the worst peril was over and he was safely in bed in the house on Sixty-fifth Street, there was only one person who did not think Roosevelt's sun had set forever at Campobello. Louis Howe said, "Franklin is still going to be president."

In a peculiar sense, the attack of polio was the best thing that ever happened to Franklin Roosevelt—it gave him what he had never had before, time to study, to learn, to think things out; and it gave him compassion. How often the world's great men have profited by a period of contemplation, from Jesus in the wilderness to Winston Churchill in political exile in his rose garden at Chartwell. Without that tragic interlude, Roosevelt might well have become president, but not a great president.

But it very nearly made him a mere Hudson River squire. The bitterest domestic battle of all was fought over his almost inert form in the houses on Sixty-fifth Street. Sara Delano Roosevelt wanted her son to retire to Hyde Park and write books—good books they might have been. Eleanor, buttressed by Louis Howe, wanted him to continue his political career whatever pain and risk it might cost him. There were high words, violent scenes, cold wars. In the end it was, of course, Franklin himself, with his invincible courage, who tipped the scales. But he could not have done it without his allies. It was, perhaps, the only battle Eleanor won over her mother-in-law, but it was the most important.

During it, Louis Howe started shy Eleanor on her own flamboyant career. "If Franklin is going to be president, you have got to keep his name before the public," he told her. "People forget so fast. You must join Democratic clubs, attend political meetings, make lots of speeches."

He taught her how to speak. She was incredibly bad. Howe raged and stormed, made fun of her, drove her to tears, then comforted and inspired her. Eleanor's first public speeches were sheer agony to her. She stuttered and blushed and felt a fool, but, in the end, she learned. How well she learned! Too well, President Roosevelt sometimes thought.

Meanwhile, Franklin was making tremendous efforts to regain control of his body and strengthen his paralyzed legs. No exercise was too arduous; no medicine too nasty; no hope too slender. It was one such slender hope that took him to Warm Springs, Georgia, and his eventual partial recovery.

Franklin Roosevelt's return to politics was signaled by his emotional speech nominating Al Smith for president at the Democratic National Convention of 1924. In it he called Smith, "The Happy Warrior," a phrase that delighted the crowd and the great radio audience. Smith did not get the nomination, but Roosevelt was once again in the political spotlight.

In 1928, Roosevelt again nominated Al Smith, who was chosen by the Democrats to run for president. In September, Roosevelt was in the swimming pool at Warm Springs when Smith called from New York to beg him to run for governor to succeed him. Roosevelt replied that he was not yet ready. Two more years at Warm Springs would enable him to throw his crutches away. Smith argued that he was the only man who could hope to carry the Empire State into the Democratic column. The other party chieftains reinforced Smith's plea. Then Eleanor came on the line and said, "I think you should do it, Franklin."

The pressure of party and personal loyalty was too much for Franklin; he agreed to accept the nomination. In the election, Smith lost New York by 103,481 votes but Roosevelt was elected governor with a plurality of 25,564. He was a vigorous, efficient governor, implementing his liberal program with sound reforms in virtually all branches of the state government. When he ran again in 1930, he was re-elected by the record-breaking majority of 725,001 votes. "That last vote was mine," he said, laughing.

The Democratic Convention of 1932 was held in the middle of the great Depression. Fourteen million workers were unemployed; the harvest rotted on the farms while people starved in the cities; business was paralyzed; banks were failing all over the country. It was not President Herbert Hoover's fault, but people wanted a change. The Democratic candidate was sure to be elected. Roosevelt was the obvious choice, but he had to fight hard to get the nomination. Ironically, Al Smith, the man he had twice nominated, was his principal rival. The pre-convention campaign was brilliantly managed by Roosevelt, Louis Howe, Jim Farley and many others. Roosevelt came into the convention with a majority of the delegates, but in those days it took two-thirds to nominate. On the third ballot, it looked as though he were stalled.

That night, Roosevelt, in Albany, slept soundly, though he doubted the outcome; Louis Howe, Jim Farley and Ed Flynn, in Chicago, did not sleep at all. All night long they were making complicated deals with John Nance Garner, who controlled Texas, and the William Randolph Hearst–William G. McAdoo forces of California. The next day Roosevelt was nominated on the fourth ballot.

Immediately, Franklin began breaking precedents. Instead of waiting to be formally notified, as was the custom then, he flew to Chicago in a chartered Ford Trimotor and made his acceptance speech to the convention, where he said, "I pledge myself to a New Deal for the American people." Though his election was a certainty, he campaigned as hard as though he were the underdog. To advise him on technical policies, he organized a group of college professors, lawyers and experts in such fields as finance, agriculture, railroads, labor and industry under the direction of Raymond Moley. Louis Howe christened it, "The Brain Trust."

In the election, Roosevelt carried forty-two of the forty-eight states. During the long interval between the November election and the March inauguration, the Depression grew worse. Unemployment rose to seventeen million. Farmers came out with shotguns to prevent the mortgages on their farms being foreclosed. Many state governors were forced to close all the banks in their states. On Inauguration Day, March 4, 1933, even the great central banks in New York and Chicago closed. If they had opened they would have been bankrupt in two hours, according to the experts. The economic life of the United States came to a dead stop.

In this atmosphere of terror and revolution, Roosevelt made one of his greatest speeches. Standing in front of the Capitol, supporting himself on the lectern, his buoyant confidence, his dynamic youthful spirit, and his strong, vibrant voice lifted the hearts of the whole nation as he said, "The only thing we have to fear is fear itself."

Coming events cast their shadows before them. That same day Japanese troops stormed the Great Wall of China. The next day Adolf Hitler's Nazi Party won an overwhelming victory in the last free election held in a united Germany.

In the first hundred days of his presidency, Roosevelt virtually reorganized the economic life of the United

States. He had brought the Brain Trusters with him, some in the Cabinet, others as personal assistants. They had prepared the bills reforming the banking system, the Agricultural Adjustment Act, Home Owners Loan Act, Emergency Farm Mortgage Act, Emergency Railroad Transportation Act, Civilian Conservation Corps (to put unemployed young men to work), Tennessee Valley Authority and the National Industrial Recovery Act which put all industry on a cooperative basis with codes of fair practices, wages and conditions of labor, even prices subject to Government supervision and planning. He also devalued the dollar, by raising the price of gold from twenty dollars an ounce to thirty-five dollars an ounce, and took the currency off the gold standard. At intervals, he explained his policies to the American people in his famous "fireside chats" over the radio. Congress gave him everything he wanted.

Other acts of social legislation, such as Social Security and taxes to redistribute wealth, followed more slowly. These drastic measures did get the economy going again, though not exactly brilliantly. There was one basic flaw in New Deal thinking. Roosevelt's economists believed that the era of industrial expansion was over; that the country would not need or be able to use any increased production for a long time, if ever. They aimed at a static, stabilized economy. Roosevelt himself thought that if the GNP (Gross National Product) ever climbed to $100,000,000,-000 a year, it would be the millennium. In 1967, the GNP topped $800,000,000,000.

Many historians and economists think that Roosevelt's drastic reforms saved the country from revolution; others hold that he started it on the road to socialism. They are probably both right. What he undoubtedly did do was to return power seized by special interests to the people and to make human rights the main concern of government.

Near the end of his first term Roosevelt lost his political mentor and best friend, the last associate who still called him Franklin. On April 18, 1936, Louis Howe, worn out by his unselfish labors, died. Almost his last words were, "Franklin's on his own now."

On his own, Franklin scored the greatest political victory of his life in November, 1936, when he was re-elected by the largest Electoral College majority since 1816. He carried all but two small states—Maine and Vermont. Congress was overwhelmingly Democratic. The great victory went to Roosevelt's head. The Supreme Court had ruled some of his pet reforms unconstitutional, especially the National Industrial Recovery Act, which was not working well in any case. The President conceived the plan of getting rid of Court obstruction by having Congress increase its membership, permitting him to appoint a new associate justice for every member over seventy years of age. Because six justices were over seventy, Roosevelt could be sure of favorable decisions by appointing six liberals to the Court. The "Court packing plan," as it was called, ran squarely into the innate conservatism of the American people. Despite the lopsided Democratic majorities in both the Senate and the House, the bill was beaten. It was Roosevelt's worst political defeat, and raised the bitterness of conservatives against him to extremes never felt before or since by a modern President. Rumors were rampant that he was insane. Even his gay laughter, that often rang out through his open office door, was described as "maniacal." This was absurd; it was sheer high spirits. In the face of all his difficulties, no man, except perhaps Roosevelt's cousin Theodore, ever enjoyed the Presidency as much.

Important as his domestic achievements were, President Roosevelt's greatest service to his country and the world was in the field of foreign policy. During his first two terms the whole world drifted with frightening speed away from democratic ideals toward dictatorship and barefaced imperialism. Mussolini in Italy, Hitler in Germany, Franco in Spain, the war lords in Japan and Stalin in Russia were in full control of events while the great democratic nations seemed paralyzed by fear. Roosevelt foresaw that the only possible counterbalance to the dictators' intent of aggrandizement by war was the United States. But the American people were blinded by the pacifistic isolationist sentiment born of their frustration and disgust at the apparent uselessness of their idealistic intervention in World War I. They were determined that never again would the new world come to the rescue of the old. Roosevelt took as his guide the maxim that "The first duty of a statesman is to educate." But he knew that it would be a difficult and delicate business.

His first move was the inauguration of the "Good Neighbor Policy" in Latin America. Secretary of State Cordell Hull was its prime mover. At first, our neighbors to the south did not believe that the United States really intended to stop interfering in their internal affairs. But such actions as withdrawing the U.S. Marines from Haiti, where they had been since 1915, and keeping hands off a series of revolutions in Cuba, convinced them that "the colossus of the North" had abandoned dollar diplomacy. Another action that pleased liberal sentiment was establishing diplomatic relations with communist Russia.

A more difficult maneuver was to revitalize the armed

forces, which were in a terrible state. The Navy had been allowed to run down; the Army was reduced to the pitiful figure of 118,000 men; and the Air Corps was flying outmoded crates. Naturally, Roosevelt turned first to the Navy. As in his day as Assistant Secretary, he greatly improved efficiency and morale. But he could not get any large appropriations for the Navy through the Congress, so he characteristically outmaneuvered the legislators by earmarking $238,000,000 of Public Works appropriations for the construction of thirty-two new warships, among them the aircraft carrier *Enterprise*. And as the war clouds in Europe grew blacker, he was able to strengthen the Army and the Air Corps.

Not until 1935 did Roosevelt really begin to devote himself to foreign affairs. Until then he had let Cordell Hull have a rather free hand. But the Constitution of the United States directly charges the President with the conduct of foreign affairs. All our strong Presidents have taken this responsibility so seriously that their Secretaries of State have been little more than glorified messenger boys. Before long, poor Hull was reduced to that status.

Mussolini's unprovoked war on Ethiopia was followed by Hitler's reoccupation of the Rhineland and his announcement of the rearming of Germany contrary to the Treaty of Versailles. Japan was gobbling up most of China except for the far-off provinces where Chiang Kai-shek held out in his bomb-devastated capital of Chungking. Roosevelt realized the danger of unchecked aggression, but he could do nothing. He asked Congress for power to embargo the shipment of arms to an aggressor. Congress replied with the Neutrality Act forbidding the shipment of arms to *any* belligerent.

In October, 1937, Roosevelt tried again. In a speech in

Chicago, the capital of isolationist sentiment, he proposed that the peace-loving nations should band together to cut off all supplies to the war-makers, to "quarantine the aggressors."

A roar of rage, a howl of anguish went up from the pacifists and isolationists. Roosevelt, they said, had been bought by "the Merchants of Death" and taking sides would mean war. Roosevelt, who subscribed to the idea that "statesmanship was doing what was possible in the right direction," knew he must drop any attempt at international cooperation and wait. And hope.

1938 was a bad year for democracy and peace and freedom. Japan continued its conquest of China and signed a tripartite treaty of alliance with Germany and Italy. Hitler took over Austria in a bloodless coup and began to move against Czechoslovakia. In October, British Prime Minister Neville Chamberlain and the French premier, in a panic, signed the Munich Pact which gave their ally Czechoslovakia to Hitler in return for his promise to make no more territorial claims in Europe. "Peace for our time," said Chamberlain on his return to London.

If Chamberlain believed that, Roosevelt did not. He understood Hitler's megalomaniacal mind as few Americans did and realized that this was another far more terrible Napoleon who would not, or could not, stop short of the domination of all Europe. With the industrial and military might of a continent under his control, would he even stop there? Roosevelt thought not. He believed that the United States, threatened on the Atlantic and Pacific, faced the gravest danger in its history. Yet his hands were tied by a neutrality-minded Congress and the divided American people. He could do almost nothing to avert the awful danger he foresaw. As he said to Congress in his State of the Union address, "This generation 'will nobly save or meanly lose the last best hope of earth . . .' "

Hitler followed Roosevelt's expectations exactly. Less than six months after Munich, he began to beat the propaganda drums against Poland, clearly the next victim. The moment of decision for Roosevelt came late in August, 1939. He was fishing from a wheelchair on the stern of the cruiser *Tuscaloosa* off the Grand Banks, when the wireless operator brought him a message. It stated that Germany and Russia had signed a treaty of non-aggression and mutual assistance. Roosevelt told the man to wheel him to his cabin and sent for his doctor, Admiral Ross T. McIntire. When McIntire had read the message, he asked, "What does it mean, Mr. President?"

Very gravely, Roosevelt replied, "It means that all the forces of despotism are now united against the weak and disunited free nations. We are the only democracy that is strong enough to halt the tide of tyranny."

Then he telephoned an order to the bridge, "The *Tuscaloosa* will proceed to New York at full speed."*

Admiral McIntire always believed that was the moment when Franklin Roosevelt decided that the United States would have to enter World War II if democracy were to survive anywhere in the world. All his subsequent actions bear this out, though not his words. For the master politician knew that he could only do what was possible in the right direction and that it would take a long time to convince the American people that, to save themselves, they must once again save the free peoples of Europe.

On September 1, 1939, Hitler's panzer divisions smashed across the Polish border. This time England and France dared not appease him. They declared war on

* Related to the author by Admiral McIntire.

Germany. Nevertheless, the conquest of Poland by Hitler took only three weeks.

Roosevelt managed to get the Neutrality Act softened to permit England and France to buy munitions on a cash and carry basis. But one unilateral action that he took in preparation for war was of far greater consequence. Early in October, Alexander Sachs, a distinguished economist and amateur scientist, called on him bringing a letter from Albert Einstein and a memorandum from Doctor Leo Szilard concerning the latest developments in nuclear fission. Sachs read the documents aloud to the President and then, in plain language, explained that the experiments pointed to the possibility of developing a bomb a thousand times more powerful than any known explosive—as it turned out, a gross understatement. Though Roosevelt knew nothing about nuclear physics, he instantly grasped the importance of the revelation and the terrible consequences if Hitler should get such a weapon first. "This requires action," he said.

Action there was. Roosevelt set up the Advisory Committee on Uranium. Within six months, the groundwork for the super-secret Manhattan Project was laid, eventually resulting in the atomic bomb. In *Roosevelt in Retrospect,* John Gunther wrote, "Here, incontestably, (Roosevelt) demonstrated one of his peculiar qualities of greatness—the capacity to see mysteriously forward, to grasp at unpredictable unknowns."

The conquest of Poland was followed by the "Phony War," six months when the armies of the Allies and Germany did virtually nothing but glare at each other from behind the great fortifications of the Siegfried and Maginot Lines. 1940 was an election year, and Roosevelt was undecided whether or not to run for a third term. Though he knew in his heart—and it was not conceit—that there was no one in either party with qualities of understanding and leadership to take his place if the situation became desperate, he was very tired. In addition, the tradition established by George Washington against a third term was a semisacred tenet to many Americans, who felt it to be a guaranty against dictatorship. Though Roosevelt delighted in smashing traditions, he did not relish tangling with that one. Hitler made up his mind for him.

In April, the German Army, without a shadow of excuse, overran neutral Denmark and Norway; in May, they poured through Holland and Belgium to attack France. Their armored divisions sliced through the French defenses with less trouble than a rotary plow through powder snow. The entire British Expeditionary Force and several French divisions were cut off in Belgium. Most of the troops were rescued by the extraordinary, heroic improvisation of British yachtsmen, fishermen and excursion boat sailors, backed by the British Navy, at Dunkirk; but all their weapons were left on the beach. In June, France surrendered. Roosevelt finally announced he would run for a third term.

Now that the Rhine was gone, the American people became uneasily aware that the frontier of freedom had, in fact, been there. The Congress gave Roosevelt virtually all he asked in the way of defense appropriations—huge increases in the Air Corps, Navy and Army; a draft law. But yet a large majority were opposed to taking a stand against the Fascist powers; neutrality and "America First" were the most popular slogans.

Great Britain stood alone against the Axis. What Americans did not know—and, fortunately, neither did the Germans—was that though the British Navy and Air Force were intact, the Army was virtually disarmed. There were no more than a hundred or so fieldpieces left in England— fewer than a hundred tanks. There were not even enough rifles or machine guns to arm the men rescued from Dunkirk. All was left on the Belgian beaches.

It takes a very great President, or a very bad one, flagrantly to usurp powers contrary to the law of the land. Roosevelt did just that. He believed, rightly, that the survival of western civilization depended on the ability of the English to defend their island home. Nothing would stop him from doing whatever lay in his power to help— nothing!

In American arsenals were about 500,000 old rifles made for World War I, and some thousands of obsolete Frenchtype fieldpieces. He sent them to England.

As the summer went on, German U-boats began taking a heavy toll of British shipping, the lifeblood of England. She simply did not have enough destroyers to protect the convoys.

This also called for action. In a remarkable piece of political prestidigitation Roosevelt negotiated a deal—if it had been a treaty, the Senate would have blocked it— whereby the United States gave Britain fifty old World War I destroyers in exchange for the use of British naval bases in the Caribbean and Newfoundland. He had no more right to do it than did dear old Mays, the black doorman at the White House. But he did, and helped to save England.

Of course, the British saved themselves. When the highly touted German Air Force tried to wipe out England's aerial defense as a prelude to invasion, the numerically vastly inferior Royal Air Force in their new Spitfires and vintage Hurricanes shot the Germans out of the sky.

The Battle of Britain was one of the great turning points of the war, and the British won it all by themselves.

But they had only won a battle, not the war. Throughout the winter of 1940–41, they grew visibly weaker as the German Air Force blasted their great cities almost to ruins and U-boats cut off their source of supplies. In addition, Britain was almost bankrupt, and soon would not be able to pay for desperately needed supplies. In a great fireside chat on December 29, 1940, Roosevelt told the American people that the United States must become "the arsenal of democracy." A week later, in his State of the Union Address, he named the "Four Freedoms" for which America must strive:

"Freedom of speech and expression—everywhere in the world.

"Freedom of every person to worship God in his own way—everywhere in the world.

"Freedom from want—everywhere in the world.

"Freedom from fear—everywhere in the world."

This speech showed truly great leadership, for it crystallized the aspirations of free men of all nations.

To get American munitions and supplies to England seemed to require either an outright gift, which Roosevelt knew Congress would never approve, or enormous loans, which would have the same baleful effect on our relations with Europe as the World War I loans. To slip between the horns of this dilemma, Roosevelt came out with a brilliant improvisation which he named "Lend-Lease." We would not lend money, but the supplies themselves. Those that were used would be regarded as expended for our own defense; unused material would be returned after the war. Because the American people were sickened by the slaughter of British civilians in Nazi bombing raids, and frightened, too, Roosevelt was able to persuade Congress to pass the Lend-Lease Bill, which, with his love of historical echoes, he numbered HR1776.

In addition, Roosevelt was giving England all sorts of extralegal help—their aviators were trained by U. S. pilots, their warships were secretly repaired in our navy yards. The Nazis did not like it, but they had too much on their hands to fight us. And in June, 1941, Hitler made the fatal mistake of attacking Russia.

Roosevelt moved one step further in August, 1941, by meeting with Winston Churchill on warships anchored in Placentia Bay, Newfoundland, where they mapped the grand strategy for the defeat of Hitler. From that meeting came the Atlantic Charter, which in essence offered the Four Freedoms to all the peoples of the world. From it also came one of the great historical friendships of all time, between Churchill and Roosevelt.

By December, 1941, we were at war with Germany in all but name; and, in the Far East, Japan was ready for her all-out attempt to dominate the Asian world. On December 7, she struck at Pearl Harbor, sinking or wrecking almost the entire American battleship fleet. In those hours of confusion and horror, perhaps the calmest man in Washington was the President. Not once in that long day and night did doubt or panic shake his nerve. He sat in his shirtsleeves in the center of the turmoil listening to reports, giving the necessary orders, thinking ahead with extraordinary clarity of mind. The next day, wearing his famous blue naval officer's cape, he drove to the Capitol and, in a magnificent speech, asked Congress to declare war on Germany and Japan.

Roosevelt's conduct of the war was inspired and inspiring. Of course, he made mistakes, as did everyone else; but wars are won by the people who make the fewest errors. Roosevelt and Churchill—a team without parallel in history—made remarkably few. For one thing, Roosevelt's choice of military leaders was extraordinarily good—Marshall, Eisenhower, Nimitz, Halsey, MacArthur. For another, his decision to win in Europe first, contrary to the wishes of many of his advisers, and the emotional urge of most Americans, including himself, was right. We could have won in the Far East and still lost in the West; but the reverse was impossible. His imaginative grasp of grand strategy and his courage in taking enormous but fruitful risks was extraordinary. Above all was the moral leadership he gave to a bewildered world.

There is no space for a point by point enumeration of important decisions, or to quote his great speeches, or even to describe the conferences—Casablanca, Teheran, Quebec (twice), Yalta—at which strategy was agreed upon, differences reconciled and policy proclaimed in inspiring messages. The point is that the disparate Allies, with their different interests and their variously armed and trained armies and navies, were coordinated and welded into a victorious union by his leadership. Though Churchill was England's greatest statesman, and in some ways more farsighted than the President, Roosevelt was the leader who united the free world by the inspiration of his words, his fairness, the gallantry of his conduct and the high humor that never deserted him.

The enormous energy the President put forth day after eighteen-hour day finally wore out his robust constitution. Toward the end of the war, his doctors ordered and all those close to him begged him to cut down his work load, to take a few months of rest. But he would not; in all truth he could not while there was still so much to do. Before he died, the war was all but won and, if the peace was partly lost, Franklin Roosevelt was not there to take the blame.

Of course, he was blamed. There will always remain those who believe that Roosevelt lost the peace at Yalta. Certainly he was ill, a dying man, though he did not himself think so for a moment, because having triumphed over death so often he was sure that he would beat it back once more and live until his role was played out. Even if, at his last conference, he did not function with the full vigor of his prime, what did he in fact "give away" to the Russians at Yalta?

Eastern Europe? The victorious Russian armies were already there; it would have taken another war to dislodge them. Berlin? It was General Eisenhower himself who proposed that the stop line for the Russian and Allied armies be fixed on the line of the Elbe River, west of Berlin. As Eisenhower pointed out to the author, at the time of the Yalta Conference, February 4 to 11, 1945, the Russians were only fifty miles from Berlin and the Allied armies were two hundred and fifty miles away and beyond the Rhine. Certain concessions to bring Russia into the war against Japan? General MacArthur urged it because he feared the Japanese would make a costly last stand in Manchuria. And the atomic bomb had not yet been tested.

Perhaps Roosevelt was too idealistic in his dealings with Stalin; it was part of his nature to trust his Allies. Also, of course, he thought he could handle the Russian dictator. Just before he died, Roosevelt began to have doubts about his own course. He was preparing to take a tougher line toward the Russians. Had he lived, the history of the peace might have been very different. For Roosevelt's enormous world-wide prestige as an idealistic liberal leader would have given him an infinitely greater leverage at the conference table than Harry Truman and Clement Atlee, the new Prime Minister of England, could command.

But, of course, he did not live. He felt so well during those early days of April, 1945, at Warm Springs; felt his strength returning in those beneficent waters as it had so often before. He was in great spirits on the morning of April 12, 1945; planning a picnic that afternoon; working on his stamp collection; looking forward to the meeting of the nations in San Francisco to organize the United Nations, the parliament of man in which he had ardently believed ever since the days of Wilson and the League.

He sat working at his stamp collection just before lunch while Madame Shoumatoff painted his portrait and his cousins, Daisy Suckley and Laura Delano, chattered gaily. Suddenly a piercing pain shot through his head. He cried out and then slumped unconscious in the chair. He suffered no more than thirty seconds and died full of great plans for the future of mankind and confident of playing a great part in bringing them about. He was very lucky. The world was not so fortunate.

The news of Franklin Roosevelt's sudden death left all the people of the world, except a few hard-core Nazis in a bomb-proof shelter in Berlin, stunned and bereft. As John Gunther wrote, "It was as if he had been President of the world."

If any American doubts Franklin Roosevelt's great services to his country let him imagine what might have been. Without his decision to go all out for atomic fission, Germany surely would have beaten us to the Bomb. Without his unilateral and extra-legal re-arming of Britain and the destroyer deal, England would have gone under in

1940. Without Lend-Lease, she would have collapsed the following year. Without his careful "education," the American people would not have entered the war in time. Without his inspired leadership, the Allies would never have been so united. And without his careful handling of Stalin, Russia might well have made a separate peace. Would any other American have dared to do those things?

Imagine, then, a world in which Hitler held all Europe *and* the British Islands, with all that enormous manpower and industrial capacity at his command. Imagine the atomic bomb in the itchy trigger fingers of that madman. Imagine Asia dominated by the Japanese warlords. Imagine the Americans standing alone against that awful concentration of military might. Imagine the incredible odds, the inevitable surrender of freedom *everywhere in the world*. And thank God for Franklin Delano Roosevelt!

3

John F. Kennedy

By LARRY G. NEWMAN

JOHN FITZGERALD KENNEDY; born Brookline, Massachusetts, May 29, 1917; son of Joseph Patrick Kennedy and Rose Fitzgerald Kennedy; educated Canterbury, Choate, Princeton and Harvard; successively secretary to his father while U.S. Ambassador in London, author, World War II naval officer, Representative from Massachusetts, Senator from Massachusetts, succeeded Dwight D. Eisenhower as 35th President of the United States, youngest man and first Roman Catholic ever elected; assassinated Dallas, Texas, November 22, 1963; succeeded in office by Lyndon B. Johnson.

Larry G. Newman, a former war and foreign correspondent for International News Service, has been for many years a Hyannis Port neighbor of the Kennedy family. He began his newspaper career in Toledo, Ohio, and went from there to become city editor of the Columbus, Ohio, Dispatch at twenty-four. For INS, he served as a correspondent in Africa and Europe during World War II and, after the war, in China and the South Pacific islands. He has also been an associate editor of Cosmopolitan, assistant foreign editor of INS and assistant to the publisher of the New Bedford and Cape Cod Standard-Times. He is now a special correspondent for United Press International and the American Broadcasting Company.

It was one of those gray, dismal mid-November Sundays in 1945. The 12:50 mass at St. Patrick's Cathedral in New York had attracted the hundreds who had slept late this day, including the tourists who had again found New York after the long, lean years of World War II, with gasoline rationing and travel problems.

Morton Downey, the singer turned business executive, and I were attending our own mass in Our Lady Chapel behind the main altar with the Rev. Fulton J. Sheen as the celebrant, still undiscovered by America's millions with television at least four full years away from maturity. Nevertheless, Sheen was not unknown as a speaker and lecturer.

As Sheen gave his last blessing and pronounced his *"Ite, missa est,"* Downey took my arm and steered me towards the back door. A tall, gaunt figure with a familiar face, eyes large, with the cast of those who have suffered long physical pain, tugged Downey's arm and they shook hands.

Outside the church, Downey said, "This is Jack Kennedy." We walked back to the Park Lane Hotel together, Downey and I, arm in arm, Kennedy a little apart.

Somehow he knew I had been a war correspondent for International News Service, perhaps because his family had always been friends with the late William Randolph Hearst, who was my boss.

Before we had walked a block, I found myself answering Kennedy's questions. Why do you think we didn't take Berlin? Could we have been in Prague before the Russians? Was Eisenhower as great as they say? What did you think of General George Patton? Were the Germans good soldiers?

It seems odd now, twenty and more years later, that the walk that Sunday morning remains so real and so vivid in memory. Yet, it shouldn't.

After Jack Kennedy left Downey and me at the door of the Park Lane and went on to his father's apartment at 200 Park Avenue, we stood to watch him go. In a few seconds, Downey said, "You have just met a man who will be President of the United States one of these days." It was said in such a matter of fact manner, I didn't doubt the truth of the prophecy.

Within a few months, Jack Kennedy started his journey to the White House by running for Congress from Boston's 11th Congressional District. In an off-election year when the Republicans took both House and Senate, Jack Kennedy became Congressman John F. Kennedy by a margin of two to one over Lester W. Bowen, his Republican opponent. That was in November, 1946.

Looking back over the years now, it might appear that John Fitzgerald Kennedy's journey to the White House was certain, easy, destined. But the story of his life from birth to death was never certain, never easy, never destined. That story is filled with pain, work, bravery and dedication to family, country and the oppressed, at home and over the world.

John Fitzgerald Kennedy was born May 29, 1917, in a rather plain but roomy house in Brookline, Massachusetts. His father, Joseph Patrick Kennedy, already had built enough of a fortune to assure his family freedom from the financial worries which troubled most first- and second-generation Irish families in Boston and other American cities in those days.

John Kennedy's mother, Rose Fitzgerald, was a Boston

beauty, the daughter of John Fitzgerald, known around the national political circuit as "Honey Fitz."

There was already one son in the house, Joseph Jr., born a year after William Cardinal O'Connell had married Joe Kennedy and Rose Fitzgerald in Boston's Cathedral in 1914. This older brother's impact and influence on Jack Kennedy's life would mold and move him until a fateful day in Dallas, Texas, in 1963.

Joe was a natural student, while Jack was not quite up to that standard. Joe was older, stronger, the leader; Jack was inclined to be one of those who catch colds easily, not exactly a dreamer but not exactly one overly interested in books and studies. Joe was the type who would run through a stone wall on the first attempt; Jack was the type who would try, over and over again.

When Joe died a hero's death in World War II, there were those who said Jack naturally moved into the path cut out for the older brother. To those who knew both, this is not necessarily true. Joe probably would have been the fortress leveler; John Fitzgerald Kennedy would have moved up to survey the damage, rebuild the city and re-assure the troubled people.

After Jack Kennedy came Rosemary, Kathleen, Eunice, Patricia, Jean, Robert, and Edward. Rosemary was different; the family recognized it from the beginning, but she had the same love and attention and even just a little more until the day came when she had to leave for a place of special attention and care.

How a family in the center of the arena matures is often the cause of gossip and speculation; so often the true pattern is misted and vague like figures in a Cape Cod fog.

Joe Kennedy, the father, was more than a bellwether; he was a father who was truly interested, deeply concerned, however busy he was amassing more and greater fortunes. Rose Kennedy was a mother in constant care and control, guiding the children in the Catholic faith (say your prayers, go to mass, respect the sacraments) but, like the father, she also taught her brood to play hard, play to win, and be fair. And also, like the father, she never taught her family to smile when they lost. That has never been an Irish trait.

Jack Kennedy never attended a public school. His father chose Dexter, Riverdale, Canterbury, and Choate. In later years when he was senator and president, John Fitzgerald Kennedy could say with that slight, serious smile, "Is it because, or in spite of them (*the private schools*)? What do you think?" He was always asking that type of question, and truly wanting an answer.

When he was elected "most likely to succeed," in his class at Choate in 1935, he asked his friend Lem Billings, "Most likely to succeed at what?"

After his graduation from Choate he went to England for the summer to study at the London School of Economics under socialist Harold Laski. But in London he came down with jaundice and his education under Laski was cut short.

In later years he could joke about that, too.

"I never thought Laski or the jaundice did me much harm," he could answer to a sharply turned question on his political leanings.

Although his father and his brother Joe were Harvard men, Jack Kennedy chose Princeton as his first university. There has been much speculation that he wanted to be out of his brother's shadow, but he once told an open forum that he chose Princeton because New York was close and there seemed to be more good looking girls around than there were in Boston and Cambridge.

Illness knocked him out of Princeton and he did wind up at Harvard after all, which may have pleased the family, especially his father, but it never appeared to impress Jack Kennedy to a particular degree.

Years later, when he was president, he would say, "Sure I have some Harvard people, but I also have some smart ones from the University of Nebraska." He liked to say that when Ted Sorenson was around. Sorenson was his speech writer and his confidant for eleven years after Jack Kennedy reached the United States Senate.

At Harvard, Jack Kennedy worked on the *Crimson,* the university newspaper, tried out for the football and swimming teams, and was no better than an average student, but he was an outstanding and well-known leader of the student body. He also injured his back in a football scrimmage; this was to influence his life profoundly.

Much has been made of the fact that President Kennedy was not a scholar in his school and university years. But one of his professors said later, "If only you could have one John Kennedy to a class, a teaching life would be almost bearable."

Of course, John Kennedy had opportunities denied all but a few at any university in any given year. He could travel, study or not study, concentrate on those areas which interested him, and send the bills home because his father and his mother had the wealth to assure him a life of ease, if he so elected.

He did not so elect. He spent his summers touring through Europe, the Europe of the 1930s dominated by Hitler and Mussolini in the West and Stalin in the East, when the United States was wracked with depression and hunger and Franklin D. Roosevelt was seeking the road back to prosperity.

From this experience came Jack Kennedy's first great literary triumph and the springboard to his later political career, *Why England Slept*. He wrote this book as a thesis in his senior year at Harvard and it stamped him, for perhaps the first time, as a student, which probably amused him.

While Jack Kennedy was at Harvard, his father was an active member of President Roosevelt's group of advisers. Joseph P. Kennedy also headed the Securities and Exchange Commission, was Maritime Commissioner, and finally Ambassador to the Court of St. James' in London. Thus the large Kennedy family were always close to government service and politics.

John F. Kennedy and Joseph P. Kennedy Jr. set their own plans aside in 1940 when they registered for the draft. On July 10, 1941, Joe Kennedy Jr. volunteered and was assigned to preliminary training as a Navy pilot at Squantum Air Station. During the same summer, John F. Kennedy, despite his Harvard football injury, lifted weights, exercised daily, played hard and studied harder because he too wanted to get into the service of his country.

The program he had laid down for himself paid off for Jack Kennedy when he was able to pass the stiff Navy physical examination. He was first assigned to intelligence work in Washington but he used every bit of his own and his father's influence to get away from his desk and into a place that promised action—the Motor Torpedo Boat Training station at Melville, Rhode Island.

But it was not until early 1943 that Kennedy shipped out from San Francisco, destined for action in the South

Pacific and the Solomon Islands. There he soon got his own ship, the PT-109.

The PT-109, with Jack Kennedy as skipper, went into action almost immediately. On Monday, Aug. 2, 1943, the PT-109 was rammed by a Japanese destroyer and sliced in two.

Back in Hyannis Port, Ambassador Kennedy received the telegram which said his son and all members of the crew of PT-109 were missing and presumed dead, or captured by the enemy.

For four days the father kept the news to himself. Then came the dramatic news over the radio that Jack Kennedy and ten members of his crew had been rescued from a small coral island deep inside Japanese-controlled territory.

Those who survived told an incredible story of Kennedy's bravery and physical endurance. From this experience, Jack Kennedy took with him a back injury, an aggravation of his old football injury, then a bout with malaria which whittled his already skinny frame down to 125 pounds. His moments without pain from that experience until his death in Dallas were rare.

Spinal surgery was performed at the Chelsea Naval Hospital in 1944 but was only temporarily successful. He had earned the Purple Heart and the Navy and Marine Corps Medal but also the burden of living with pain and disappointment.

In early September of that year, Jack Kennedy also suffered another staggering blow. His older brother, Joe Jr., was lost in a low-level bombing mission in an air strike against German installations on the English Channel. Thus was passed the torch from Joe Jr. to Jack Kennedy.

Almost his first duty as the older brother was a sad trip

to New York to comfort his sister, Kathleen. Her husband, the 26-year-old Marquis of Hartington, had died in action in France. A few years later, Kathleen herself died in a plane crash, another crushing blow to the closely knit Kennedy family.

Despite the tragedy in the family and his own physical condition, Jack Kennedy was not deterred from setting out on the journey which would lead to the White House.

His victory in the 11th Congressional District was won through dogged campaigning door to door, from dawn until midnight. His back pain often forced him to use crutches, but he discarded them to walk the stairs of the three-story tenements in the 11th District. His victory was considered a minor upset by the old-line politicians, but he formed his pattern of campaigning and organization and awed even those Boston ward heelers.

He was re-elected to Congress in 1948 and again in 1950. In 1952, with characteristic disregard for the old-line political thinkers, Jack Kennedy decided to challenge Henry Cabot Lodge for a seat in the United States Senate.

Lodge was a proven vote getter in Massachusetts. He had turned back the challenge of such political figures as James Michael Curley, David I. Walsh and Joseph Casey. Lodge was so confident that he told Arthur Krock, the New York *Times* Washington bureau chief, that he would beat Jack Kennedy by at least 300,000 votes.

Kennedy's campaign rolled across the Commonwealth of Massachusetts attracting huge crowds to "tea parties" and early morning coffee "klatches." Lodge's campaign was more leisurely and was hampered from the outset by overconfidence. The knockout blow against Lodge came in September when Basil Brewer, publisher of the influential

New Bedford and Cape Cod *Standard-Times* dailies, gave his and his newspapers' support to Kennedy.

Governor Adlai E. Stevenson of Illinois, the Democratic nominee for president, came into Massachusetts to campaign for himself and for Jack Kennedy. Rarely, in American politics, had two such articulate men worked toward a common goal.

But, on election day, Stevenson was overwhelmed by General Dwight D. Eisenhower; yet Kennedy defeated Lodge by a margin of 70,727 votes. Basil Brewer's influence was felt in the New Bedford area where Kennedy polled 37,350 votes to only 15,812 for Lodge.

Lodge was later to say, "It was those damned tea parties which licked me." Less biased and equally astute political observers said Kennedy's victory was due more to the shift away from the old-line politicians and to a new breed who had the energy and courage to fight the established order.

It has been said John Kennedy's career in his early days in the Senate was short of spectacular. But the record shows he was not afraid of loaded questions, national or international.

He talked about trade with Poland at one Overseas Press Club luncheon and, later in 1956, at the annual dinner, spoke of Algeria and colonialism, another political red hot potato.

In 1959, he wrote the author of this chapter a letter dealing with civil rights. "I am in full agreement with you," he said, "that this tragic episode illustrates again the need for a stronger civil rights act. [*He was discussing the lynching of Mack Charles Parker in Mississippi.*]

"Two years ago, I voted for the retention of Title III in the Civil Rights Act, and I favor the enactment of that Title still.

"Senate Bill 810 which has been introduced by Senator Douglas [of *Illinois*] does offer an opportunity for Congress to put into effect those additional protections of civil rights which were defeated in 1957. I want to assure you that this is a matter which has my full attention and that I intend to vote for a strong civil rights bill."

It was in defeat that Jack Kennedy was thrust into the national spotlight. In 1956, Adlai Stevenson was again the Democratic nominee for president, but he threw the fight for the vice-presidency open to a floor battle in Chicago.

In one of the most exciting battles in national convention history, Kennedy fought the late Estes Kefauver for the second place on the ticket. There was a lot of shifting and maneuvering during the vote, but Speaker of the House Sam Rayburn was to tell me later, "When you have the gavel, you see the hands you want to see."

"Mr. Sam" helped defeat Jack Kennedy for the vice-presidency, but Kennedy's place in the party's future was assured in a brief but eloquent speech he made supporting the Stevenson-Kefauver ticket and promising there would be "other times in other years."

Kennedy was re-elected to the Senate in 1958 and, for the first time in memory, a Democrat carried Cape Cod. His state-wide victory over Vincent J. Celeste was an incredible 874,608 votes, the greatest victory ever given a candidate in Massachusetts history, Democrat or Republican.

On January 2, 1960, Senator Kennedy announced he would be a candidate for the Democratic nomination for President.

But that had been known all along. I recall a telephone call one night from Palm Beach, Florida, where he was resting during the holidays. I had asked him to speak at the annual dinner of Sigma Delta Chi at the Hotel Plaza in New York.

He asked me in that telephone conversation, which lasted more than an hour, "Who will be there?"

I said Ed Murrow, Walter Cronkite, Bob Considine, General David Sarnoff, Bill Paley and mentioned a lot of other names which I figured would influence his decision.

He was impressed, but the question he asked which stopped me cold was, "Yes, I know all of them, but how many delegates will be there?"

"None," I guessed, "with the possible exception of James Farley, the former postmaster general."

"After the nomination and election I will consider it another time. But right now I have to go after delegates every minute of the day and night I am able to move," he answered, and that concluded the discussion.

His old back injury was troubling him, but he had decided against another operation such as the one in 1954 which brought him again to death's door. He had determined to live with the pain and a minimum of medication. He was silent in his suffering and rarely confided in anyone, including members of his own family, when the pain put him back on crutches for periods of time.

His nomination in Los Angeles in 1960 was almost a foregone conclusion despite the belated efforts of Senator Lyndon Johnson and Speaker Rayburn to derail the Kennedy drive. Senator Johnson joined the ticket over the protests of Rayburn and others who would have preferred Richard Nixon to Kennedy in the White House.

The matter of Kennedy's Catholic religion had been widely discussed prior to the convention. It was a major issue the day after the Kennedy-Johnson ticket set out on the road leading to the White House.

Kennedy decided to meet the issue head-on even though he felt it an insult to be questioned about it. It was about the only question which could bring the anger to his face and the knife to his voice.

In the final analysis it was his determination to surface the religious issue that changed many voters' minds. The televised debates, he later said, were a factor, but he felt his facing up to the religious question brought support from those who feared—and ofttimes hated—Catholics.

After his election over Nixon, he told a group of reporters at his Hyannis Port home that "if nothing else I hope this election has brought this country of age on the matter of religion."

Throughout the campaign, Joseph P. Kennedy Sr. had stayed in the background. He later was to say, "Hell, I don't want them voting against me. Jack has a mind of his own and I'm not able to change it very often these days." Other members of the family, however, worked day and night. Robert and Edward, Eunice Kennedy Shriver, Patricia Kennedy Lawford, Jean Kennedy Smith, and the nominee's mother, Rose, joined the thousands who became part of Kennedy's battle.

The night before the election, Jack Kennedy told me, "It will be close, a battle all the way. I think I'll win but it certainly will be no landslide."

He had correctly analyzed the situation. He felt President Eisenhower's late entry into the Nixon campaign had closed some of the gap the Kennedy-Johnson team had built.

On the evening after his election, most of the news reporters were invited over to the Hyannis Port "compound." The President-elect was asked what we should call him now. He said he thought "Senator" was correct until he took office. After that, none of those who knew him well ever called him anything but "Mr. President."

It was on that same evening after his election that he heard of a back injury which had been bothering Peter Lisagors of the Chicago *Daily News*. The President-elect made arrangements for the newsman to see his doctor in New York, Mrs. Janet Travell. He placed the call personally—on the night of what must have been his greatest triumph. But he knew pain well, and he immediately thought of sharing with a friend some release which he had found in Dr. Travell's treatments.

That morning, he had gone to the Armory in Hyannis with Jacqueline Kennedy and other members of the Kennedy family. Jacqueline was awaiting her second child; her first, Caroline, stayed home. His few remarks that day concluded with, "So now, my wife and I prepare for a new Administration and for a new baby. Thank you."

When all the votes were finally tallied, Kennedy had defeated Richard Nixon by a mere 112,881 votes. This worried him, he told friends, and he added that so many wounds had to heal, so many tempers be calmed, so many feathers smoothed, he supposed he would have to move slowly on controversial subjects.

John Jr. was born a few months later to bring great joy to the President-elect. Those who knew Jack Kennedy over the years knew his great love for his own children, and for all children for that matter. When, later on, the burdens of office weighed heavily in those early days of his presidency, the Bay of Pigs, the Berlin Wall, the confrontation in Vienna with Nikita Khrushchev, in the back of his mind, the President said, "I keep thinking of what kind of world we are going to turn over to our children."

His inaugural address was one of the most moving and

dramatic in the nation's history. He lashed out at the old fears and the new ones and he summoned all men to help.

"The energy, the faith and the devotion which we bring to this endeavor will light our country and all who serve it—and the glow from that fire can truly light the world.

"And so my fellow Americans: Ask not what your country will do for you—ask what you can do for your country.

"My fellow citizens of the world: Ask not what America will do for you, but what together we can do for the freedom of men."

His inaugural address lasted but fourteen minutes, yet its message sent a fire of pride burning through the country. Despite the closeness of the election, John Kennedy had managed to bring the country closer, and the bitterness of the campaign was soon lost.

Around the world, however, he was tested. The Bay of Pigs, which he inherited, was a frightening debacle. He took the blame, but he learned a lesson.

"You just can't have government by consensus," he said later in a private conversation. "The President must walk alone and make the lonely decision." He did that often after the Bay of Pigs.

His early programs had been dreams long before he went to the White House. The Peace Corps, the Alliance for Progress, more federal aid to education, all had been the subjects of late evening discussion in the years before he reached the White House.

When the missile crisis in Cuba came, in the early winter of 1962, Kennedy did not take counsel of his fears, nor listen too long to his multitude of advisers. The Bay of Pigs was too fresh in memory. He knew defeat in this crisis might well be his end and the end of the free world.

The President ordered ships of the U.S. Navy to ring

Cuba and he sent the Air Force over in strength. He told the Russians to get their missiles out of Cuba or face military action.

Khrushchev, who had blustered and boasted at the Vienna conference, now faced a president who no longer listened to bluster and boast. Khrushchev backed down, the missiles were taken back to the Soviet Union and President Kennedy had avenged his earlier insults and defeats.

There were other battles before and after, the crisis at the University of Mississippi, the civil rights battles in the streets of the South, churches bombed and burned, and murder. The President ordered the Justice Department to enforce the law as drawn up in the civil rights bills the Congress had passed but which had gone almost forgotten until Kennedy moved.

Because of the preoccupation with crisis, President Kennedy's "New Frontier" program had rough sledding in Congress. Some of his pet measures got through, others gathered dust in Congressional bins as 1963 came.

President Kennedy's popularity had grown, the religious issue was dead, and he welcomed another campaign. "We need a mandate from the voters," he said one evening in Hyannis Port. "I know we'll get it in 1964. The country is moving again, our people have confidence in themselves and their Government again. There is pride again in what we have been, what we are, and what we can be." He was like an evangelist when selling his country, its goodness and its strength.

Mrs. Kennedy was expecting another child, and the President was worried but happy for her and for his other two children. In August, 1963, Patrick Bouvier Kennedy was born at Otis Air Force Base on Cape Cod. The struggle for life lasted but a few days. It was one of the rare times that President Kennedy ever showed his emotions in public.

The death of his son, the prolonged illness and paralysis of his father, were blows which would have shattered the strongest. But President Kennedy had learned through his faith to accept tragedy, pain and other anguish and disappointment. That day at Otis Air Force Base, as he arrived back from Boston, where his young son had died after the short struggle for life, President Kennedy's face was written deep with sorrow. He stopped at the door of Mrs. Kennedy's suite for a moment, brushed a tear from his eye, smoothed the shock of hair from his forehead and walked inside. When he returned to take Jacqueline Kennedy home, he looked older but more serene than we had seen him in months.

Early that fall, in October, he made a trip to New England to honor his old friend, Robert Frost. He stopped in Hyannis Port, on his way back to Washington, for a short visit.

We chatted that evening on a Hyannis Port street about the upcoming election, about his brother Edward's career in politics. He was excited with the old 1960 fire now.

A few weeks later, he was gone.

The historians will have the chore of evaluating John Fitzgerald Kennedy as a congressman, a senator and as President of the United States.

Those of us who knew him will never live quite as fully again. I see him on board the destroyer *Joseph P. Kennedy* at the America's Cup races; in the Hyannis Port harbor grounding his Wianno Senior, *The Victura,* and arguing he was not at the helm; I see him in church, at St. Francis Xavier in Hyannis. Who could forget the morning he turned to Eddie Folliard of the Washington *Post* and Mae Craig and Connie Hurley of the Associated Press and whispered, "Have you ever given it a thought that if someone tried to shoot me, they'd get one of you first?"

Jacqueline Kennedy was able a year after his death to write of him, as few have been able to write before or since:

"Someone who loved President Kennedy, but who had never known him, wrote to me this winter: 'The hero comes when he is needed. When our belief gets pale and weak, there comes a man out of that need who is shining—and everyone reflects a little of that light—and stores some up against the time when it is gone.'

"So now he is a legend when he would have preferred to be a man. I must believe he does not share our suffering now. I think for him—at least he will never know whatever sadness might have lain ahead. He knew such a share of it in his life that it always made you happy whenever you saw him enjoying himself. But now he will never know more—not age, nor stagnation, nor despair, nor crippling illness, nor loss of any more people he loved. His high noon kept all the freshness of the morning—and he died then, never knowing disillusionment."

4

Jonas Salk

By DOROTHY DUCAS

JONAS EDWARD SALK; born New York City, October 28, 1914; son of Daniel B. Salk and Dora Press Salk; educated New York public schools, College of the City of New York and New York University College of Medicine; after receiving medical degree, successively research associate in epidemiology and assistant professor of epidemiology University of Michigan School of Public Health, assistant research professor in bacteriology and head virus research laboratory University of Pittsburgh, research professor in bacteriology Pittsburgh, professor of preventive medicine Pittsburgh, Commonwealth professor experimental medicine Pittsburgh and director and fellow Salk Institute for Biological Studies; resident La Jolla, California.

Dorothy Ducas first met her subject when she served as public relations director of the National Foundation for Infantile Paralysis, which sponsored the research leading to the discovery of the Salk vaccine. A graduate of the Columbia University School of Journalism, she was the youngest woman ever to receive a Pulitzer traveling scholarship. She has worked as a reporter for the London Sunday Express, New York Herald Tribune, New York Post and International News Service. She was an editor of McCall's and, during World War II, she founded and headed the maga-

69

zine bureau of the Office of War Information. She is a recipient of the "Headliner Award" of Theta Sigma Phi.

WHEN THE SUMMER SUN grows warm and children swarm to beaches and swimming pools, parents today can watch them without the nagging fear that suddenly, without warning, the healthiest and most robust among them might be stricken by the crippling disease of polio. Polio now is merely the name of one of the protective shots children take in infancy.

But, until 1955, summer was the "polio season," a time when ambulances screamed in the night, playgrounds and beaches closed, isolation wards were filled to overflowing somewhere in the United States, year after terrible year. Parents were gripped with fear that their children might die, have to live in iron lungs or never walk again without crutches and braces, like the late President Franklin D. Roosevelt.

That fear was wiped out by a young doctor named Jonas Edward Salk, who developed the first preventive vaccine against poliomyelitis, also known as infantile paralysis.

Contrary to legend, scientific discoveries do not spring into being, like Athena fully formed from the brow of Zeus. Medical heroes such as Edward Jenner, discoverer of vaccination against smallpox, and the immortal Louis Pasteur struggled for many years before their discoveries were accepted. Jonas Salk has joined their company. But in the twentieth century everything moves more speedily. Salk's struggle ended in victory before he was forty-one.

The development of the Salk vaccine was a modern miracle, like penicillin or anesthesia. But it was unique in medical history because it was a *planned* miracle. Jonas

Salk did not create it alone. His was the final, brilliant achievement in a research program supported by millions of Americans through the National Foundation for Infantile Paralysis, founded by Mr. Roosevelt after he became President.

Salk has said he could never have done it without the earlier work of other scientists, the advice and support of medical committees, the Foundation grants and the driving force of its lawyer-president, Basil O'Connor. For saying this Salk is called modest. But he never has underrated the importance of his achievement. His faith in his own work carried him through years of grueling battle.

Jonas Salk never wanted to be a hero. When the renowned Dr. Thomas Francis Jr., of the University of Michigan, announced results of the field trial of the Salk vaccine in Ann Arbor on April 12, 1955, Jonas was proud that he had proved his point: a killed-virus vaccine could produce reliable protection against paralytic polio. As whistles blew and sirens sounded, people went to church to bless his name and, later, when a grateful world showered him with honors, he was embarrassed. He wanted the end of paralytic polio and the respect of his peers. He had a distaste for the fanfare that surrounds a public figure in today's world. Never was there a more reluctant hero.

On that day in Ann Arbor, Edward R. Murrow, the late television commentator, told Jonas, "Young man, a great tragedy has befallen you . . . you have lost your anonymity." Salk never has regained it. He has lived in the goldfish bowl of publicity, bathed in an aura of adulation he never sought and still views uneasily.

Salk was born anonymously enough, the eldest of three sons of humble parents in the East Harlem area of New York City. His father, Daniel, was a shirtwaist factory worker, never affluent. His mother, Dora Press Salk, was the traditional Jewish mother, strong-minded and intensely ambitious for her children. They moved to the Bronx when he was quite young. Jonas went to school with other children of immigrants. He was a skinny, small-boned boy, nearsighted enough to need glasses while still young. He was not an expert athlete, although today he swims quite well and plays golf. He obtained good grades without being a "grind" and was accepted at Townsend Harris High School and the College of the City of New York, both of which required exceptional ability as a requisite for entrance.

He never had a burning ambition to "be somebody," like most storybook heroes. Instead, his goal was independence in his thinking and his work. He yearned to do things in his own way, not subject to the commands of higher-ups. And, most of all, he wanted to contribute to the society in which he lived.

He was not a "born" doctor. He thought first of becoming a lawyer, because lawyers fought injustice. But his introduction to science in college changed his direction.

At twenty, he entered New York University Medical School, where he said from the start he never intended to go into private practice. Research held the fascination for him that wider horizons held for Columbus. He dreamed what seemed to him then the improbable dream of making medical discoveries of benefit to mankind. Even among his test tubes and sacrificed mice, rabbits and monkeys, people were always of prime concern to Jonas Salk. He regarded social obligation as one of the requisites of a good scientist.

At the end of his first year in medical school, Salk took a year's leave as a biochemistry fellow. Because of this early training (he even published a professional paper on a new technique for concentrating bacteria) he was better qualified than most young doctors in the field of immunology. In his senior year—was it fate or just coincidence?—his mentor was Dr. Francis, then chairman of the bacteriology department at NYU.

Jonas was graduated in 1939 and, the next day, married Donna Lindsay, whom he had met at Woods Hole, Massachusetts, while working in the laboratory there to help pay his way through medical school. Although his mother had scraped together $1,000 for his first year, Jonas earned his way through college like any Horatio Alger hero. Donna, a Smith graduate, was attending the New York School for Social Work. Her interest in overcoming injustice was even more intense than his.

As an intern in New York's Mt. Sinai Hospital, Dr. Salk proved an able physician and surgeon. His bedside manner was warm and sympathetic; it still is, when he is called upon by friends and associates in an emergency or as it was when he gave thousands of children his polio vaccine with a gentleness that neutralized the sting. He remained in touch with Dr. Francis during his internship; his goal always was the laboratory, not the bedside.

Like so many born and bred New Yorkers, Jonas and Donna wanted to stay in their native city. Yet Mt. Sinai and the Rockefeller Institute both turned him down when he sought a job. Ironically, the man who refused him at Rockefeller was Dr. Thomas M. Rivers, dean of American virology, chairman of the National Foundation Virus Research Committee that later granted millions for his vaccine work.

The National Foundation began to play a role in Salk's life that same year. He received a National Research Council fellowship to work with Dr. Francis at the University of Michigan, where Francis had become head of the department of epidemiology. The Council was administering a program funded by the National Foundation for Infantile Paralysis. Jonas did not even know this then. Later on, the National Foundation could boast about having financed part of Salk's education, as well as his vaccine work and he never objected. Although his attitude toward publicity was skittish, like most research scientists, he was always grateful to the National Foundation. The humanist side of him appreciated that partnership between medical and lay people offered a new vehicle for getting things done.

Salk left Ann Arbor—after five and a half years and promotion to an assistant professorship—to head a new virus research laboratory at the University of Pittsburgh. Here, he thought, was a real opportunity for independent work. His new laboratory, understaffed and cramped, had hardly got going when Harry Weaver, research director of the National Foundation, visited him in the basement of the Pittsburgh Municipal Hospital, where polio patients were cared for on upper floors. To Weaver, the location was perfect for the virus-typing program, with a source of virus available on the spot.

The program itself was a routine, tedious job, necessary for the eventual making of a vaccine, despite the fact that well-established virologists had no desire to engage in it. To Jonas, it meant larger laboratory space, more staff and $200,000 a year with which to work in a new field, polio. He attacked the project with vigor. True to form, he began having some original ideas almost at once. The methods by which the three known types of polio virus were to be identified—and others, if they existed—seemed to him cumbersome and slow. He suggested another way.

His suggestion was vetoed at a Virus Typing Committee meeting, at which Dr. Albert Sabin of the University of Cincinnati rebuked him for bringing the question up. He made Salk feel like a presumptuous newcomer. The professional and personal battle of these two March-of-Dimes-supported polio vaccine developers may be said to have dated from that time.

Salk did the typing by his own method anyway, then had his staff corroborate the findings according to committee specifications. This gave Salk time to start his own polio immunization research.

To his surprise and delight, he was chosen to report on the typing program at the Second International Poliomyelitis Conference in Copenhagen. There, the great Dr. John Enders of Harvard, in reviewing his non-nervous tissue culture method for growing virus, mentioned that Dr. Salk had immunized laboratory animals with virus grown in test tubes. The statement brought from Dr. Sabin a prompt warning about "undue optimism." The two adversaries now were out in the open.

With a new grant for his research at Pittsburgh, Dr. Salk attacked the many technical details of growing virus, treating it with formalin in just the right amount, at the right temperature and for the right length of time. Always the innovator, he began using monkey kidney tissue on which to grow the virus, instead of monkey testes, which had been used before. This, he found, increased the yield. He knew vast amounts of virus would be needed for a vaccine to protect humans.

His detractors began to talk about vestiges of monkey kidney getting into the vaccine and possibly causing human kidney damage. They said Salk's inactivated vaccine would not produce high enough antibody levels in the bloodstream. They doubted his assertion that only a small amount of antibodies was needed because infection created instant increase. And, over and over again, as he worked eighteen-hour days, skipping lunch and dinner, he heard the chant of orthodoxy, "A live virus-vaccine is the only way to produce immunity."

His opponents, including Dr. Sabin, were capable and respected scientists, who attacked the principle of killed-virus vaccine from honest conviction, to be sure. But they represented tradition, not innovation. And the outspoken Dr. Sabin was working on a live-virus vaccine himself, so his charges at medical meetings and press conferences looked to the outside world like professional jealousy.

All through the period of deliberation as to whether to try the killed-virus vaccine in human beings, it was Sabin who persistently undermined the growing optimism. Salk did not press for a nationwide trial. With the caution of a true scientist and a conscientious human being, he wanted to test every aspect again and again. But he never faltered in his belief that his vaccine would work.

The first inoculations of his experimental vaccine were given to children at the D. T. Watson Home in Leetsdale, just outside Pittsburgh, in June of 1952. He gave it in the safest possible way, only to children who had had polio and whose blood he had typed. So he knew which of the three polio viruses had attacked each child and gave shots of the *same type* to which they already had immunity. Bleedings later showed a marked rise of antibody of *that* type. It worked!

"Still," said Dr. Salk, "when you inoculate children with a polio vaccine, you don't sleep well for a number of nights."

There might have been side reactions. A child might

have been allergic to the needle itself. Anything could have happened which, if known, would have discredited the vaccine without real cause. Nothing happened. Nor did it when Dr. Salk took the next step, inoculating those who had *no* antibodies to begin with. They, too, produced high levels.

The marvel was that nobody found out about these first experiments. More than two hundred parents and staffs of several institutions knew about them, but so earnestly had Dr. Salk explained the need for secrecy that, to a man, they held their tongues. Later, it became known Dr. Salk had vaccinated his own three sons and his wife. What greater faith could a man have in his untried product?

Announcement of the experiment was to be made in the traditional way by publication of a paper in the *Journal* of the American Medical Association of March 28, 1953. Then Salk's luck ran out. A Broadway columnist blared the news in advance: "New Polio Vaccine—Big Hopes Seen." Salk was upset. He did not want people to expect too much too soon. Summer was approaching. He must tell them the truth: the vaccine could not be ready even for testing in 1953. How could he make sure his message got through to the people without false optimism or equally misleading discouragement?

He elected an unprecedented step for a scientist. He would go on the radio in a special program entitled "The Scientist Speaks for Himself." He hoped to exert a moderating effect on public reaction, without damage to his scientific reputation.

"We want to reach our goal as quickly as possible," he said. "This objective will be achieved if we move cautiously and with understanding, step by step. Certain things cannot be hastened, since each new step cannot be

made without establishing first the wisdom of the one before. We are now faced with facts, not merely theories. We
can now move forward more rapidly and with confidence."

As with every innovating step Salk took, the reaction
had repercussions he had not intended to provoke. The
public received his report calmly. Their faith in him was
strengthened. But the popularity that burst into frenzy a
year later can be said to have started at that time. He was
besieged by reporters, photographers, film makers. His
telephone never stopped ringing. It was a month before he
could calm his nerves sufficiently to go on injecting volunteers. And, of course, his radio appearance was regarded by
the medical world as undignified and unprofessional.

In retrospect, it is amazing that even as the vaccine was
being made and tested by five pharmaceutical firms, Salk's
own laboratories and the National Institutes of Health, the
young scientist had to devote so much of his time and
energy to relatively extraneous matters. There were problems of monkey shortage, vaccine potency and safety tests
to which he wanted to devote his whole mind. The field
trial was being planned, with clashing opinions as to its
pattern. These, to him, were the important matters. Yet he
had to fight for time to think about them.

Dr. Salk preferred to have half a million children in the
first three grades of school vaccinated, then, after the
summer, have their attack rate compared with unvacci-
nated children in the same grades. There was strong feeling, even within the National Foundation, that what is
known as the "double blind" method provided the only
truly controlled study. In it, half the children would receive vaccine, the other half a harmless fluid known as a
"placebo." No one would know who got which until results were compared.

The system finally decided upon was a combination of the two. In some states there were injected controls, in others merely observed controls. For when Dr. Francis was persuaded to direct the field trial, he insisted on the double-blind method he had used in his flu vaccine trials in 1943–44. Salk went along. The redoubtable O'Connor simply said, as he had for years, "Scientific decisions must be made by scientists."

We at the Foundation began readying a flood of information material for the health authorities and volunteers in counties where children would be given their shots, we hoped, at the end of April. Interest was high. Despite overwork, everything seemed at last to be progressing. Then, early in April, another blow was struck. Walter Winchell, gossip columnist, announced over the air that the new polio vaccine was not safe! It had killed monkeys! The Michigan Medical Society had pulled out of the field test!

The Vaccine Advisory Committee was meeting in White Sulphur Springs at the time. You can imagine what consternation reigned. The members knew it was misinformation, of course. A prompt press release was issued explaining that all vaccine was being tested in monkeys and if any contained live virus, it was being discarded. The Winchell "tip" had come from the medical writer, Paul de Kruif, who had no part in the vaccination program but a keen nose for news. Michigan later came back into the trial. But, in the meantime, many laymen were alarmed.

"Will this frighten parents into withdrawing their children from the field trial?" Jonas asked me that night.

I wanted to reassure him, but all I could say was: "Yes, for a while. But not enough of them to ruin the trial."

Undoubtedly, many children were withdrawn. But

1,830,000 participated, of whom 651,000 were subjected to the needle.

On April 26, 1954, the trial began, the day after another photo-finish meeting of the Vaccine Advisory Committee in Washington. National Institutes of Health scientists were worried by what they believed were brain lesions in monkeys injected with Salk vaccine.

It took the last-minute expert opinion of Dr. David Bodian of Johns Hopkins to relieve them of their unwarranted fears by certifying the lesions were unrelated to the vaccine.

The public never knew how difficult it was to make that "go" decision. The night before the vote was taken for the start of the largest medical trial in history, every Committee member searched his soul.

"I think the vaccine is okay," one of them told me. "But nobody can *know*. What if a dozen healthy children are paralyzed?"

They voted unanimously to go ahead next day, while reporters waited anxiously in a hotel press room. I found Jonas Salk biting his fingernails on a bench outside the meeting room.

"Why aren't you in there?" I asked.

"They are voting now," said Jonas. "It's not my decision to make."

When the first polio pioneers lined up for their shots all over the country, Dr. Salk's ordeal should have ended. He had no responsibility for the trial; Dr. Francis was in complete charge. He wanted to go back to Pittsburgh and work. Still there was no privacy, no lessening of pressure. And the attacks on his vaccine continued, even while over one-half million children carried it in their bloodstreams.

At the Third International Poliomyelitis Conference in Rome in September, 1954, Dr. Sabin outlined his progress with the live-virus vaccine, now almost at the human trial stage. Concurrently he brought up the question of monkey kidney damage through use of the inactivated vaccine in humans. Dr. Bodian and Dr. Salk challenged his implication. Dr. Sven Gard of Sweden also declared he had made vaccine according to the Salk recipe and found live virus in it. Salk told him if it had live virus it wasn't his vaccine.

"Something was done differently," he declared.

There he was, on the verge of proving his principle, still boxing and ducking the blows of detractors. It continued throughout the waiting period. Salk felt like Ignaz Semmelweis, who conquered childbed fever by getting obstetricians to wash their hands. He told Richard Carter, his biographer (*Breakthrough: The Saga of Jonas Salk*) :

"They had never washed their hands and resented my telling them to do so. Albert [Sabin], in effect, was legitimizing their attitude by assuring them that we shortly would provide a means of delivering babies safely, without washing the hands."

When the time came for the conclave of scientists and doctors to hear the Francis Report in Ann Arbor, Jonas was a weary man. I met him and his family at the airport the day before. No committee was there to greet him. No photographs were taken except by a Foundation associate. All attention was turned to Dr. Francis, who knew the answer to the big question: "Does the Salk vaccine work?" But Salk did not seem nervous. In his heart he knew the verdict would be favorable. He thought of Ann Arbor as the end of a rugged voyage he would be glad to have over.

"I actually thought I'd go to that meeting, hear the report, read a paper of my own, talk to a few newsmen and return to Pittsburgh and my laboratory the next day. I was totally unprepared for what happened at Ann Arbor," he told Carter.

What happened was that he became a hero. He emerged that day as a white knight with a tiny vial of pink fluid to save future generations from the dragon of crippling polio. The man who had protested that the vaccine should not even bear his name was a living legend. Like folk heroes of other times, his was a household name.

There was a story going the rounds then about a little Jewish boy who came home from school and asked, "Mama, was Davy Crockett Jewish?" His mother, smiling, answered: "No, dear, but Jonas Salk is."

Salk also was an acknowledged public figure. President Dwight D. Eisenhower awarded him (and O'Connor, too) the United States Medal for Merit; he received the Lasker Award, the Criss Award, countless citations and plaques. Schools and streets were named for him. His picture was on magazine covers, television screens and in textbooks. In 1965 he and the National Foundation were honored with a Joint Resolution of Congress expressing the gratitude of the nation on the tenth anniversary of the introduction of the Salk vaccine. He won all the popularity contests in which the public could vote. But he has never received the Nobel Prize nor membership in the National Academy of Sciences. Both these groups depend on recommendations from other scientists.

The final blow was the Cutter incident, a polio epidemic afflicting over two hundred people, caused by defective vaccine from one manufacturer. The public never was given a full account of the reasons for that tragedy, which obviously resulted from inexact following of Jonas Salk's protocols. Vaccinations were suspended; then, one by one, the manufacturers' procedures were reviewed and production was resumed. Cutter Laboratories chose never to make polio vaccine again. The incident cut Salk to the quick. Again he did not sleep well at night. The final elimination of paralytic polio was set back several years.

Even so, outbreaks were lessening, figures on cases receding. By 1961, before any appreciable amount of Sabin vaccine had been used, polio incidence had dropped by 97% from its 1950–54 average.

The Sabin attenuated vaccine was endorsed by the American Medical Association before it was available for use, a hitherto unheard of act. That august body even urged mass vaccinations with it under AMA leadership, a procedure Salk and O'Connor had urged for Salk's vaccine in 1955. Why? It was a live-virus vaccine in which doctors persistently believed. Also, it was given orally on a lump of sugar, thus was much easier and cheaper to administer to masses of people.

But if it was regarded as safer than the Salk vaccine, a rude surprise awaited. Type I Sabin vaccine was licensed in August of 1961, Type II in October. Type III was not released until Spring of 1962. There were misgivings about evidence of stability of this type in trials conducted, of necessity, in the Soviet Union, because susceptible children were too few in the United States by then. Live "tamed" virus, you see, can revert to its wild state as it passes from person to person. During the four months following its release, sixty-two cases of Type III polio actually were reported in adults who had taken it. The Public Health Service eventually advised those over eighteen not to take it routinely.

Jonas Salk might have gloated at his arch-rival's vaccine

troubles, had there been a trace of meanness in his character. He did not.

Both vaccines are in use today and both are as safe as careful manufacture, testing and constant surveillance can make them. One wonders, now, why this could not have been achieved without so much skepticism, antagonism and trial by fire for pioneer Salk.

Yet perhaps the in-fighting, the constant need for interpretation of his ideas and even his public acclaim served a good purpose in the end. They schooled him to take a giant step in response to a far wider challenge, the creation of the Salk Institute for Biological Studies.

Salk today is devoting his life to a new concept: the combination of science and the humanities capable of someday improving human beings as a whole. History books of the future may yet remember Salk best for having been the world's first "bio-philosopher."

The Salk Institute in La Jolla, California, became a reality in 1964. There biologists, chemists, physicists and mathematicians are working under one roof to apply the most advanced insights and technologies of the life sciences to all of man's ills—and at the same time to relate their discoveries to human values. In the near future social scientists will join the faculty, for, in the Salk view, molecules and morals are as interrelated as air and water.

Backed by the enthusiasm of his friend and adviser, Basil O'Connor, who is, if anything, even more enthusiastic about the significance of the Institute than he was about the conquest of polio, and with annual financial support from the National Foundation—March of Dimes, as well as other sources, Salk already has achieved an operating complex of 140 people, 96 of whom are engaged in research. In a perfect setting for the pursuit of knowledge, six distinguished resident fellows are devoted to exploring the "new biology."

Relieved from teaching duties and administrative responsibilities, with laboratories designed to meet their individual needs, these men work side by side, with consequent cross-breeding of their special interests. Each has a "meditation tower" in which to consider the implications of his work. It is the only center of learning of its kind in the world and, indeed, the first cooperative scientific community in history.

Its initial work is in molecular or cellular biology, that new discipline in which complete understanding of the living cell is sought, with the purpose of eventually controlling the complex structure of cells that is man.

Salk has always been concerned that man is able to release the power of the atom but not the potential of man. By the fusion of science and the humanities, Salk believes ways will be found to prevent unconquered infectious diseases, premature heart and blood vessel disease, cancer, hereditary diseases and allergies; to repair and transplant human organs; to reduce the ills of aging and to prolong man's useful life span.

The resident fellows are Edwin Lennox, former physicist who helped develop the atom bomb, now working in genetics; Renato Dulbecco, virologist, whose special interest is cancer; Leslie Orgel, chemist, concerned with the chemical origins of life; Melvin Cohn, biochemist and biologist, who is studying the mechanisms by which the body fights infection; and Jacob Bronowski, mathematician, whose chief concern is the effects of science on our culture.

In addition to the residents, there are five non-resident fellows who spend varying amounts of time each year at the Institute. They are Jacques Monad, of the Pasteur Institute in Paris, who shared a 1965 Nobel Prize for exploration of genetic materials; Warren Weaver, vice-president of the Rockefeller Foundation, top scientific administrator and planner; Jerome Wiesner, Dean of the School of Science at Massachusetts Institute of Technology, interested in applying physical and electrical sciences to the new biology; Francis C. Crick, physicist turned biologist, who shared a Nobel Prize for discovery of the basic structure of DNA, the essential genetic material; and Salvatore Luria, Professor of Microbiology at MIT, a pioneer in molecular biology.

Dr. Salk is director of the Institute, but he is also a resident fellow. His laboratory is investigating auto-immunity, the phenomenon by which the body produces antibodies to its own parts; this may lead to new knowledge about arthritis, multiple sclerosis and thyroid disease. He also is studying the mechanism by which the body rejects or retains grafts, tumors or transplanted tissues, the big problem in heart and kidney transplant surgery today.

Walter Cronkite recently said in a Columbia Broadcasting System television program, "The 21st Century": "In the past Salk worked on diseases which attack the body from outside, like polio. Now he is concerned with those which attack from inside."

Will lightning strike twice? Will there emanate from the Institute a single vaccine for prevention of all virus diseases? A prevention of cancer? Of birth defects? A technique to prevent rejection of human tissues? No one knows, nor will they for many years. But if any one of these happened, Dr. Salk would become, all over again, a scientific hero.

He still flinches at that word, but he has mellowed. The

awe in the voices of strangers he encounters nowadays touches rather than embarrasses him. He is too intent on his new, enormous goals to protest.

He explained it himself on the CBS television program:

"I sometimes think that the idea of creating an institute was to create a shelter for myself. I still hope, because in me hope seems to spring eternal, that I can somehow, some way, find a refuge here, find respite from the strong tendency and temptation and desire from others to have me function as a public figure rather than as an individual. These two kinds of lives are mutually incompatible. Perhaps I have not fought as successfully as I might have, but I'm hoping one of these days I can—within myself at least—win the battle."

5

Mahatma Gandhi

By MARGARET BOURKE-WHITE

MOHANDAS KARAMCHAND GANDHI; born Porbandar, India, October 2, 1869; educated India and University College, London; admitted to the bar and practiced law in South Africa, gave up law to fight against anti-Indian legislation there, abandoned Western ways and practiced Hindu ideals of asceticism, developed concept of civil disobedience expressed in nonviolent resistance to the laws, returned to India as Nationalist leader, given title of Mahatma (great soul) by people, campaigned against British rule by fasting, sole representative of Indian National Congress at London Round Table Conference on India, major figure in conferences leading to India's independence and partition, campaigned against violence between Hindus and Moslems; assassinated New Delhi, January 30, 1948.

Margaret Bourke-White was in India when Gandhi was murdered. A distinguished photographer, she began working as an industrial photographer in 1927 and has taken photographs in twenty-four countries and the Arctic. Once an associate editor of Fortune, *she has been with* Life *magazine since it began and has served as a war correspondent in Great Britain, North Africa and Europe. Her photographs are in the collections of major museums, and she is the author or co-author of a dozen books.*

MANY PEOPLE have asked me if I could tell, when in the presence of Mahatma Gandhi, that this was a truly great man. The answer to that question is *Yes,* one always knew. There seemed to be an aura hanging over Gandhi. A touch of magic clung to this little brown man with his squeaky voice which influenced opinions around the world.

Gandhi had many peculiarities. He considered orange juice, tea and milk of the cow, a sacred animal, as stimulants; he permitted himself only goat's milk. Believing as he did in the simple life, Gandhi, when he traveled, always went third-class on the train. But third-class cars in India are as jammed as New York subway trains during the rush hour, so special arrangements had to be made. On big trips a whole group of third-class trains were taken over by Gandhi and his followers. Because Gandhi had renounced cow's milk, it was essential for the goats to go along on these trips. The goats also traveled third-class.

I was reminded of a remark made by Mrs. Sarojini Naidu, the celebrated Indian poet, who said, "If only Gandhiji realized how much it costs to keep him in poverty."

On one of these trips I was the only unattached woman accompanying the expedition. A small coffin-shaped compartment was slipped into place for me. The compartment just ahead of me carried Prime Minister Nehru, the compartment behind carried Gandhi and his goats. This gives me the distinction, I'm sure, of being the only woman ever to have slept between Nehru and Gandhi—with goats thrown into the bargain.

Gandhi had been educated at London University. He

spent the first years of his professional life as a lawyer in Durban, South Africa, where many Hindus lived. Gandhi was appalled to see the restrictions and often cruelties which the Hindus had to suffer, and this brought him into active work for them after he went back to his home in India. He took the helm at once and found a potent weapon in nonviolence.

The scenes of rioting against the British Empire were a little like our own struggles in America against racial discrimination. There is one high point where Gandhi and his followers were in direct revolt in an episode a little bit like our Boston Tea Party. With Gandhi it was not tea, but salt; the pattern was a familiar one. Gandhi and his followers took part in giant demonstrations against the government salt monopoly. First, they cut out salt from their food; second, they marched to the sea and made their own salt by evaporation.

Gandhi had many idiosyncrasies. One was his weekly day of silence. For six days he talked a great deal, then, on Mondays, he observed strict silence. Gandhi neither held nor wanted any government office, but was consulted on every important question that came up in the fight for freedom. There were freedom talks in full tilt when I was there as a correspondent.

My insatiable desire to be on the scene when history is being made was never more nearly fulfilled than on my visit to India. I arrived there in 1946 when India stood shining and full of hope on the threshold of independence. I witnessed that extremely rare event in the history of nations, the birth of twins, Pakistan and India. I had an historical drama to photograph, with a full cast of characters, including villains and one of the saintliest men who ever lived. And when the saint was martyred, I was near.

Gandhi's death marked the end of an epoch. I was privileged to record its final two years. They were the key years, covering the vital cumulative period with its various clashing forces.

Whenever Gandhi took up residence in Bombay he stayed with the untouchables, the very poor of Poona on the bottom of India's caste system. Usually, Poona, Gandhi's headquarters, was like the inside of a blast furnace. Gandhi, whenever he stepped outside his hut, looked like a great mushroom on legs under the huge, wet Turkish towel he wore heaped and dripping on his head. Despite the heat, the untouchables' colony was a sort of summer White House, with cabinet ministers, maharajahs and dignitaries of all sorts pouring through the gates.

There was one dignitary who went his own way. That was Mohammed Ali Jinnah, the Qaid-i-Azam, or "great leader" of the Muslim League. He had a razor-sharp mind and hypnotic, smoldering eyes. It would be hard to imagine two men more different than Jinnah and Gandhi. They sat at opposite poles at just the time when India, moving forward into freedom, needed unity.

Gandhi stood for a united India for everyone. Jinnah insisted on a separate Pakistan for Muslims. Though non-religious himself, he raised religious differences to the heights of fanaticism. He inflamed the masses with his fiery words, goading them to frenzy. Under it all, he was a spear of ice.

Jinnah masterminded the situation so adroitly that within months he was to win his Pakistan. He said, "We will have either a divided India or a destroyed India." Immediately following this announcement, violence broke out in Calcutta. I flew there from Bombay and found a horrible scene, the dead and dying strewn about in the

streets and numbered high in the thousands. They had
traveled a long road to freedom, these peasants and shop-
keepers, both Muslim and Hindu, who had struggled side
by side for independence from the British Raj. In a city
larger than Detroit, vast areas were dark with ruins and
black with the wings of the vultures that hovered impar-
tially over the Hindu and Muslim dead. Like Germany's
concentration camps, this was the ultimate result of racial
and religious prejudice.

The terror in Calcutta set off a chain reaction which
spread through the country and was equally devastating to
both religious groups. Months of violence sharpened the
division and highlighted Jinnah's arguments. On August
15, 1947, one year after the riots in Calcutta, a bleeding
Pakistan was carved out of the body of a bleeding India.

It took me two years to appreciate the greatness of
Gandhi. It was only in the last act of the drama, when he
stood out so bravely against religious fanaticism and
prejudice, that I began to glimpse his true greatness. He
was an extraordinarily complex person, with many contra-
dictions in his nature.

Some of his opinions I found difficult to reconcile. One
was his opposition to industry and scientific agriculture.
That an emergent nation like India needed modern industry seemed to me self-evident. It seemed to me that
tractors were just what India needed along with irrigation
dams. India's tired, eroded strips of land, her dependence
on the vagaries of the monsoon for water—these were
desperate land problems that cried out for scientific agriculture.

Gandhi closed a gap between the Middle Ages and the
twentieth century. This was a source of his strength. His
roots were in a simple pre-machine era. He grew up in a

period when machinery was something that the foreign power possessed and developed at the expense of its colonial subjects. The raw materials India's people produced were sent out to feed machines on the other side of the world. To Gandhi, in his boyhood, the machine must have been the enemy. To him, in his seventy-eighth year, it was still the enemy.

I shall never forget my first visit. I went to see him in Poona. Having thought of the Mahatma as the symbol of simplicity, I was a bit surprised to find that I had to go through several secretaries to get permission to photograph Gandhi. I then discovered that I would not be allowed to see the Mahatma until I had learned to spin. "Don't you know how to spin?" asked Gandhi's secretary.

"Oh, I didn't come to spin with the Mahatma. I came to photograph the Mahatma spinning."

"How can you possibly understand the symbolism of Gandhi at his spinning wheel? How can you comprehend the inner meaning of the wheel, the *charka,* unless you first master the principles of spinning?" he inquired sharply. "Then you are not at all familiar with the workings of the spinning wheel?"

"No. Only with the workings of a camera."

The secretary fell into rhapsody. "The spinning wheel is a marvel of human ingenuity. The *charka* is machinery reduced to the level of the toiling masses. Consider the great machines of the factories, with all their complex mechanisms . . . and consider the *charka.* There are no ball bearings; there is not even a nail."

"You will make me drop photography and take up spinning," I said politely.

"That is just what I wish you to do," said Gandhi's secretary.

"How long does it take to learn how to spin?" I asked wearily.

"Ah," said the secretary, "that depends upon one's quotient of intelligence."

I found myself begging for a spinning lesson.

"I must compose editorials for Gandhiji's weekly magazine, *Harijan*," said the secretary. "I have a deadline to meet. Come back again next Tuesday."

Somehow I persuaded Gandhi's secretary that my spinning lesson must start this very afternoon. It embarrassed me to see how clumsy I was at the wheel, constantly entangling myself. It did not help my opinion of my own I.Q. to see how often and how awkwardly I broke the thread. I began to appreciate as never before the machine age, with its ball bearings and steel parts, and maybe an occasional nail.

Finally, my instructor decided I could spin well enough to be brought into the presence of the Mahatma. There were two injunctions I must faithfully follow. I must not speak to the Mahatma, as this was Monday, his day of silence. And I must not use any form of artificial light, as Gandhi disliked it. I could see from the outside that Gandhi's hut was going to be very dark indeed.

I found the inside of the hut even darker than I had anticipated. A single beam of daylight shone from a little high window directly into my eyes. When my eyes became accustomed to the murky shadows, there sat Gandhi, cross-legged, a spidery figure with long, wiry legs, a bald head and spectacles. Here was a man who was leading his people to freedom and who had kindled the imagination of the world, the Mahatma.

The only sound was a little rustling from the pile of newspaper clippings he was reading. I was grateful that he would not speak to me because this was his day of silence. However, I would make another appointment with him for later.

Then Gandhi pushed his clippings aside, and pulled his spinning wheel closer. He started to spin, beautifully, rhythmically and with a fine nimble hand. I set off a flash-bulb. I could tell instantly from the span of time from the click of the shutter to the flash of the bulb that my equipment was not working properly. The heat and moisture of India had affected all my equipment. My next picture worked beautifully until I glanced at my camera and noticed I had forgotten to pull the slide. The third was successful; I threw my arms around my equipment and sailed out into the daylight, quite unsold on the machine age.

The secretary was waiting outside, all smiles. I had been in the "presence"; I belonged. He asked graciously if I would like to see a demonstration of spinning on Gandhi's own personal spinning wheel—the portable one he carried when he traveled.

"I would enjoy that very much," I replied. I enjoyed it even more than I had anticipated, for, in the middle of the secretary's demonstration, the spinning wheel fell to pieces. That made me feel better about the machine age.

This was the first of many occasions on which I photographed the Mahatma. Gandhi, who loved a little joke, had his own nickname for me. Whenever I appeared on the scene with camera and flashbulbs, he would say, "There's the Torturer again." But it was said with affection.

In the case of Gandhi, I came to see this episode about the spinning wheel in a different light. To Gandhi, the spinning wheel was laden with meaning. For millions of

Indians it was a symbol of the fight for freedom. Gandhi played an important role in the freeing of Indian women when he led his demonstrations against the British Empire. He brought these shy, and in some cases veiled, Indian women out into the open. They marched with him and waved banners very much as street demonstrators in any country would. Gandhi instructed them to destroy anything that would bring the British a profit; he organized an enormous boycott. He induced women by the thousands to join him on his nonviolence parades. He instructed them to destroy every hat of British manufacture that they could find. It was an odd sight to see these women jumping up and down around bonfires, snatching hats from people's heads and throwing them into the flames.

Gandhi's evening prayer meetings gave him a great pulpit from which to comment on any subject, large or small. The crowds who came at twilight to hear him ran into thousands; his listeners into millions, as his prayer talks were broadcast each day. At prayers, Gandhi gave the people homey little hints on health and diet, advising mothers to give their babies mudpacks for whatever ailed them. He instructed villagers that the wooden plow was more sacred than the tractor. He denounced the machine, saying that it would create a nation of slaves. He sometimes delivered a special diatribe against textile machinery.

The anti-machine references at prayers always disturbed me, especially since they were delivered through a modern microphone. When the talk was finished, Gandhi would step off his prayer platform into the milk-white Packard car belonging to the richest textile manufacturer in India, Mr. Birla, who had supported Gandhi and his followers for over thirty years. Of course, Gandhi took nothing for himself, and the members of his ashram lived in austerity. But yet I was not satisfied by these inconsistencies.

Despite all her difficulties, India was raising herself from the debris of an out-worn order and was drawing up a democratic constitution. The new laws abolished untouchability and opened schools to the untouchables. New laws do not automatically dissolve old inequities, but literacy speeds the process. This was an interesting time to be in India.

The coming of industrialization would be a powerful democratic influence. People of all castes and all sorts would work together and rub elbows. A machine cares nothing about a man's ancestors; it does not feel polluted by his touch, knows no prejudice.

The splitting of India into two nations, based on religious antagonisms, had increased the deadly hatreds and fears. Muslims caught on the Indian side of the new borders and Hindus caught on the Pakistani side were fleeing their ancestral homes in incredible numbers. All roads between India and Pakistan were choked with endless convoys of peasants and their bullock carts. Women rode on donkeys; men walked, often carrying the very young or very old on their shoulders.

There were heartbreaking subjects to photograph. Babies were born along the way; people died along the way. Thousands perished. I saw children pulling at the hands of their mother, unable to understand that those arms would never carry them again.

The terrible chain of events stirred Gandhi, in Delhi, to action of his own nonviolent kind. He chose a weapon which was peculiarly Asian, and had brought him spectacular successes in the past. He announced at prayer meeting that he would undertake a fast directed against the savageries of religious warfare.

This would be the sixteenth fast of Gandhi's life. He was now seventy-eight and it could be his last. The previous fifteen had been directed against the British Government, but this fast was against the inadequacies of the new all-Indian government, which he had done so much to create. Being a Hindu himself, Gandhi found it intolerable that other Hindus should be massacring the Muslim minority. When Hindu refugees began storming Muslim mosques in Delhi, throwing out Muslim worshipers and moving their own families into these holy places, Gandhi felt the moment for action had come.

With this sixteenth fast, Gandhi was launching the hardest battle of his life—the battle to conquer inner hatreds. His method of nonviolence had led his people to independence. Now he was faced with the more difficult task of winning tolerance and unity.

It is difficult for a Westerner to understand the significance of a fast. I called on Pandit Nehru, who I was sure could help me understand. "Voluntary suffering," said Nehru, "has great effect on the Indian mind. Gandhi is a kind of sentinel who stands apart. The fast does two things; it introduces a sense of urgency to the problem, and forces people to think out of the rut—to think afresh."

Next morning, there was a little ceremony for which Gandhi's closest followers gathered. I was within arm's length of the Mahatma while he took his last mouthful of boiled beans, his last sip of goat's milk, and placed on the cot in front of him his famous dollar watch. The hands pointed to eleven. The fast had formally begun. Some of his followers began to cry.

Many people came to prayers that night in the garden,

and waited in uneasy silence for Gandhi to speak. He began talking very simply about the reasons for the fast—how all people deserved equal protection and equal freedom of religious worship, and emphasized that there must be no retaliation against acts of violence. "How long will I fast?" asked Gandhi. "Until I am satisfied that people of all religions in India mix like brothers and move without fear; otherwise, my fast can never end."

As he talked, I thought, it is really himself he has on trial. He has a religious position of his own to defend—his belief in the brotherhood of man, which is just as essential to Hinduism as it is to Christianity. His whole philosophy of nonviolence is at stake. He is pitting all the strength left in his thin, wiry body against the spirit of hate consuming his country. One could sense his power to call on the people's inner strengths, for he was closer to the soul of India than any other man. I believe that everyone who went to prayers that night had a feeling that greatness hovered over the frail little figure talking so earnestly in the deepening twilight. "I am not alone," were his closing words. "Because although there is darkness on the way, God is with me."

During the tense days that followed, the Mahatma became too weak to go to prayers in the garden. The people were clamoring for a sight of Gandhiji, and one day they were allowed to line up by twos and file through the garden at the back of Birla House, where Gandhi was staying. The doors of the porch were open. Gandhi's cot had been set between them, and on it lay the little old man, asleep.

I find it hard to describe my feeling at seeing this frail little figure lying there, with the silent, reverent people filing by. It would be impossible to imagine such a thing in America—a prominent person asleep and yet on exhibition to his public. There is an extraordinary amount of personal intimacy in the attitude of Indians toward their leaders. I have never seen it in any other country.

From then on, the public began taking a hand in the fast. Every hour saw an increase in the processions, in the formation of peace brigades, and massing together for open-air meetings. On the fifth day of the fast, there was a mammoth meeting at Urdu Park, which had packed all the wide meadows stretching between the historic Red Fort and the bubble-shaped domes of the Jamma Mosque. Thousands had gathered on the grounds around Birla House when Nehru arrived. Sensing the temper of the crowd, he climbed to the top of a cement gatepost by the drive to speak. Nehru's eloquence was legendary, and I was glad to spot in the crowd an Indian newspaperman friend who could translate. "If our goal is good, the path to it should be righteous. If we want to be free, we must free each other first. Only a free people can lay the foundation to a free land," Nehru was saying. "These are the lessons of Gandhiji."

It was growing darker in the garden, and then something very beautiful happened. Hundreds of bicyclists turned their lamps on Nehru, and the garden seemed to be flickering with fireflies. "It is a sustaining thought," Nehru continued from his gatepost, "that there is something great and vital in the soil of our country which can produce a Gandhi, a personality of his character, even though a Gandhi may be born only after a thousand years."

It happened I had a dinner engagement with Nehru that evening. I hurried back to the hotel to change my clothes and rejoined him at his home. I remember my embarrassment at having changed to evening dress for what turned out to be a simple and very informal dinner. As I rose from the table to leave, Nehru got word that Gandhi's physical condition was alarming. All through the night, an astonishing range of religious leaders, who had never approached agreement before, were working on a peace program.

Early next morning, I went to Birla House and learned from Gandhi's happy followers that the Mahatma had received what they called a "spate" of telegrams. At exactly eleven o'clock on the sixth day, Gandhi broke his fast. It was a moving experience to be there and see the people laughing and crying for joy. Gandhi lay smiling on his mattress on the floor, clutching some peace telegrams in his long, bony hands. I jumped up to a high desk and got my camera into action. Gandhi's daughter-in-law rushed in with a tall glass of fruit juice, and he kissed her. Then Pandit Nehru, who was sitting by his side, made a little ceremony of holding Gandhi's glass of orange juice for him.

Then the women followers flocked in carrying trays of orange slices, which Gandhi blessed. This was "prasad," food offered to God. The women passed the fruit platters to the crowd, even handing up bits of orange to me, where I stood taking pictures, so that the foreigner, too, could share in the gift offered to God.

Gandhi's fast had aroused great soul-searching among the people. For a time, the violence died down. Certainly many problems remained unsolved. But Gandhi's heroic risking of his life had stirred the entire country, and the people bent their will toward peace.

But there were some exceptions. The militant society of fanatically orthodox high-caste Hindus known as the Hindu Mahasabha was vigorously opposed to everything

Gandhi stood for. Through what they called an "awakening race spirit," they dedicated themselves to the return to the pure Hinduism of two thousand years ago, with its superior privileges exclusively for Brahmins. The society had its own youthful storm troopers, Rashtrya Savek Sangh. This reminded me of the youth movement in Germany—the savage Hitler Jugend. Oddly enough, the R.S.S. also used the swastika as their emblem, an ancient Indian symbol which far antedated Hitler.

Race supremacy theories cannot live with tolerance; therefore, a Hindu leader who flouted caste and advocated equality and brotherhood had to be destroyed. Several days after the termination of Gandhi's fast, a homemade bomb was thrown at him from the wall during prayers. Fortunately it fizzled out without hurting anyone. Gandhi reacted in a purely Gandhian manner. He assured his listeners at prayers that he held no malice against the poor, misguided youth who threw the bomb. He hoped the young man would realize his error, for it was a wrong done to Hinduism and to the country.

I had reached my last day in India, and on this final day I had arranged a special treat for myself—an interview with Gandhi—because although I had photographed him many times, and we had exchanged scraps of conversation with one another, I had never had a chance to sit down and talk with him quietly.

I found Gandhi seated on a cot in the garden, with his spinning wheel in front of him. He put on a big straw hat when I arrived, to keep the sun out of his eyes. It was a hat someone had brought him from Korea, and he tied it at a gay angle under his chin. I told Gandhi that this was my last day, and explained that I was writing a book on India, and wanted to have a talk with him before I went home.

"How long have you been working on this book?"

"It's almost two years now."

"Two years is too long for an American to work on a book," said Gandhiji, laughing. He began to spin, as he always did during interviews.

My first question seemed a rather silly one at the time; later, it seemed almost prophetic. "Gandhiji," I said, "you have always stated that you would live to be a hundred and twenty-five years old. What gives you that hope?"

His answer was startling. "I have lost the hope."

I asked him why. "Because of the terrible happenings in the world. I can no longer live in darkness and madness. I cannot continue. . . ." He paused, and I waited. Thoughtfully, he picked up a strand of cotton, gave it a twist and ran it into the spinning wheel. "But if I am needed," he went on in his careful English, "rather, I should say, if I am commanded, then I shall live to be a hundred and twenty-five years old."

We went on then to speak of other things, such as how to improve the condition of untouchable children, and how to bring about land reform. I questioned him about his attitude toward machinery in general. Was he positively against the use of science and machines in agriculture? He assured me that he was. While frequently I did not agree with Gandhi's point of view, talking with him helped me understand it. Gandhi cared not at all about reshaping the structure of society. He cared a great deal about reshaping the human heart, and calling out the best in every man.

I turned to the topic which I most wanted to discuss with Gandhiji. I began speaking of the weight with which our new and terrible nuclear knowledge hangs over us, and of our increasing fear of a war which could destroy the world. Holding in our hands the key to the ultimate in violence, we might draw some guidance, I hoped, from the apostle of nonviolence.

As we went on speaking of these things, I became aware of a change in my attitude toward Gandhi. No longer was this merely an odd little man in a loincloth with his quaint ideas drawn from a bullock-cart culture—certain of which I heartily rejected. I felt in the presence of a new and greater Gandhi. My deepening appreciation of Gandhi began when I saw the power and courage with which he led the way in the midst of chaos.

I asked Gandhi whether he believed America should stop manufacturing nuclear weapons. Unhesitatingly, he replied, "Certainly America should stop."

Gandhi then was pre-occupied with the importance of choosing righteous paths, whether for a nation or for a single man; for bad means could never bring about good ends. He spoke thoughtfully, haltingly, always with the most profound sincerity. As we sat there in the thin winter sunlight, he spinning, and I jotting down his words, neither of us could know that this was to be one of his last messages to the world—perhaps his very last.

Never had I felt his peculiar greatness more strongly than on this day, when the inconsistencies that had troubled me dropped away, and Gandhi began to probe at that dreadful problem which has overwhelmed us all.

I asked Gandhiji how he would meet the atom bomb. Would he meet it with nonviolence? "Ah," he said. "How shall I answer that? I would meet it by prayerful action."

I asked what form that action would take.

"I will not go underground. I will not go into shelters. I will go out and face the pilot so he will see I have not the face of evil against him."

He turned back to his spinning, and I was tempted to ask, "The pilot would see all that at his altitude?" But Gandhi sensed my silent question.

"I know the pilot will not see our faces from his great height, but that longing in our heart that *he* should not come to harm would reach up to him, and his eyes would be opened. Of those thousands who were done to death in Hiroshima, if they had died with that prayerful action—died openly with that prayer in their hearts—the war would not have ended as disgracefully as it has. It is a question now whether the victors are really victors or victims." He was speaking very slowly, and his words had become toneless and low. "The world is not at peace." His voice had sunk almost to a whisper. "It is still more dreadful than before."

I rose to leave, and folded my hands together in the gesture of farewell which Hindus use. But Gandhiji held out his hand to me and shook hands cordially in Western fashion. We said goodbye, and I started off. Then something made me turn back. His manner had been so friendly. I stopped and looked over my shoulder, and said, "Goodbye, and good luck." Only a few hours later, on his way to evening prayers, this man who believed that even the atom bomb should be met with nonviolence was struck down by revolver bullets.

I was only a few blocks away when the assassin's bullet was fired. News travels with lightning swiftness in India, and in a few minutes, I was back at Birla House. Thousands of people were already pressing toward the scene of the tragedy. The crush was so great, I could hardly reach the door, but the guards recognized me and helped me through. In the next moment, I was in the room where Gandhi, dead less than an hour, lay on a mattress in a corner on the floor. His head was cradled lovingly in the lap of his secretary; the devoted little grandnieces and daughters-in-law who had always surrounded him in life clustered around him now as he lay in his last sleep.

I remembered the joyful moment when he had broken his fast only ten days earlier in this very room. I had stood in this very spot and watched him smile up from this same mattress. Then everyone had been laughing for joy. Now they were silent and stunned. Few people even wept. The only sound was the endless chanting of the "Gita" by the women followers who sat along the edge of the mattress and swayed to the rhythmic recitations of the "Song of God," always sung at the death of a Hindu. The women kneeling along the mattress were beating their hands softly to the rhythm of the prayer.

Suddenly into the numbness of that grief-filled room came the incongruous tinkle of broken glass. The glass doors and windows were giving way from the pressure of the crowds outside, straining wildly for one last look at their Mahatma, even in death. No one expected Mahatmaji would die, even during the fast, or when the home-made bomb was thrown during prayers. And now that death had come, the sense of personal loss was almost beyond endurance.

I pressed my way through the grief-stricken crowd to the garden path where Gandhiji had met his end. The place was marked off with a humble little line of sticks, and a large and very ordinary tin can about the size of a large jam tin had been put down to indicate the exact spot where he fell. Already a radiance hung over the spot. Someone had marked the place with a candle. And kneeling around it were men and women of all religions, just as Gandhiji would have had it. United in deepest sorrow, they were reverently scooping up into their handkerchiefs small handfuls of the blood-stained earth to carry away and preserve.

I was swept by the crowd back to the gates, and there I found Nehru speaking. Once more, he had climbed up on the gatepost of Birla House to address the people. "The great light is extinguished," he said. "Mahatmaji is gone, and darkness surrounds us all.

"I have no doubt he will continue to guide us from the borders of the Great Beyond, but we shall never be able to get that solace which we got by running to him for advice on every difficulty."

At this point, Nehru broke down and wept openly on the gatepost, and the crowd wept with him. Then he made a supreme effort to speak a final sentence. "We can best serve the spirit of Gandhiji by dedicating ourselves to the ideals for which he lived, and the cause for which he died."

All through that terrible night, people gathered in hushed groups in the streets. In the morning, I would have pictures to take, and broadcasts to think of. But this night, I gave myself over to walking the streets, sharing the shock and sorrow of the crowds. Within hours, the police had captured the assassin, Nathuram Vinayak Godse, a fanatical Brahmin, editor of a Hindu Mahasabha weekly in Poona. Later he would be given the death penalty. But to those masses of bereaved people, it was not merely one misguided individual who had murdered their Gandhiji, but an impersonal force that had dealt out death.

In this, they were very right. It was no accident that Gandhi was done away with by a fellow Hindu—one of those who stood for all that was worst and most rabid in the religion, just as Gandhi stood for all that was broadest and best.

By dawn, the lawn and gardens of Birla House and all streets leading into it were flooded with people. By the thousands they swirled through the Birla gates until they crushed in an indivisible mass against the house. And still they came, beating against the walls of the house in surging waves of mourning humanity. I doubt if there has ever been a scene like it. Certainly there has been none in my experience. The house, its concrete terraces, was like a rocky island, holding its precious burden high above the sea of grief. Laid out on the roof of the terrace was the figure of Gandhi, tranquil and serene.

The morning sunlight lent a special radiance to the coarsely woven homespun which draped his body. He was carried down, placed on a flower-laden bier and covered with the yellow, white and green flag of the new free India. Then, the greatest of all processions began to move toward the sacred burning ground on the bank of the River Jumna. The human stream gathered to itself all the tributaries of the countryside. It grew and grew until it was a mighty river miles long, and a mile wide, draining toward the shore of the sacred river. People covered the entire visible landscape until it seemed as if the broad meadows themselves were rippling away until they reached the sacred banks. I never before had photographed or even imagined such an ocean of human beings.

Somehow I managed to get to the center of the dense, mourning throng, where the funeral pyre of sandalwood logs had been lighted. Occasionally I could catch a glimpse of the three Hindu priests kindling the fire and scattering perfumed chips on the blaze. Then a glimpse of Nehru's haggard face as he stood by the edge of the bier. Twilight was coming. The flames were rising high into the sky. All through the night, the people would watch until the flames burned down to embers.

The curtain was falling on the tragic last act. The drama I had come to India to record had run its course. I had shared some of India's greatest moments. Nothing in all my life has affected me more deeply, and the memory will never leave me. I had seen men die on the battlefield for what they believed in, but I had never seen anything like this: one Christlike man giving his life to bring unity to his people.

6

Eleanor Roosevelt

By FANNIE HURST

ANNA ELEANOR ROOSEVELT ROOSEVELT; born New York City, October 11, 1884; daughter of Elliott Roosevelt and niece of Theodore Roosevelt; active in social work, married Franklin D. Roosevelt, author of syndicated newspaper column, assistant director Office of Civilian Defense, U.S. delegate to United Nations, chairman of UNESCO Commission on Human Rights, author of six books; died New York City, November 7, 1962.

Fannie Hurst completed her story on her old and good friend, Eleanor Roosevelt, on February 19, 1968, four days before she died at the age of seventy-eight. The author of many famous bestselling novels, including Back Street *and* Imitation of Life, *she came to New York from Hamilton, Ohio, to become one of the best-known women of her day. Like Mrs. Roosevelt, a great humanitarian and worker in causes, she served as a United States delegate to the World Health Organization.*

EVERY NOOK and corner of the Eleanor Roosevelt personality has been explored and evaluated, except perhaps the tiny mosaics of her every-day humanness, that shine like tiny chip-diamonds through her grandeur.

Be that as it may, only time, which creates its classics, will determine the ultimate evaluation. Mine, however, persists. Eleanor Roosevelt was one of the first, if not the first, ladies of the world, the list exotic and highly limited.

Yet this great lady was something of a paradox. She was not an intellectual; she belonged to no high-level establishment, but far beyond, she operated through intelligence, her humanness and humanity infallible.

Her education was that of an average well-bred girl of social status, adequate, but extended by a gift that seldom failed her. Eleanor Roosevelt was an out-and-out brain picker, which largely no doubt accounted for her talent for concentrating on whatever she might be doing at any given moment. She listened to statesmen and mendicants with equal intensity and grilling interest. Whoever you were, patient in a hospital ward or Maharajah, you became the centrifugal force of her thinking. She cared.

I frequently accompanied her through hospital wards. Every bed became the focus of her concentrated attention. Her compassion needed to know the details of each case.

These ingredients of personality, simple and uncomplicated, nevertheless account for the noble stature which this young girl of high level but lonely upbringing was to achieve.

Eleanor Roosevelt grew into her greatness. After an orphaned but carefully nurtured girlhood, well schooled privately in the United States and France, the girl who married her cousin, the highly eligible Franklin Delano Roosevelt, man of destiny, did not presage the ultimate woman who was to emerge from the baptism-of-fire years that followed.

First, of course, were the child-bearing years, always under the domination of an overpowering mother-in-law, who had never cut the umbilical cord that bound her son to her and who was to spread darkly the immensity of her maternal wings over the young wifehood of her daughter-in-law.

The emergence of Eleanor Roosevelt from her imprisonment in those early years dates from the shattering circumstance of Franklin Roosevelt's poliomyelitis. It was subsequent to this calamity that a clarion call sounded with Eleanor, and, almost instantly, she became legs and messenger for a husband who was to remain almost chairbound for the historically meaningful years of his life.

The nation reacted variously to this emergence from housewife into world activities, mostly critically. What is the big idea, the first lady of the land gallivanting over the country? Woman's place is in the home, commandingly so when that home happens to be the White House.

Long before I became excitingly involved with the Roosevelt administration, as far back as my college years, I wrote Eleanor Roosevelt, then wife of the governor of New York, praising her attitude with regard to improved conditions for domestic help. Shortly after, I arrived in New York from the middle west, just another literary aspirant seeking the great cultural center for the disposition of my pen-and-ink wares.

A few months later, I found myself marching beside her in a Fifth Avenue parade of the League of Women Voters and our friendship seemed to spring full-grown into life.

I was not only to come to regard the relationship as the most inspiring of my entire experience but to revel in the gaiety and the humanness of this woman who, hour by hour, was growing, along with her husband, into a contemporary figure of destiny.

She was not only aware of the immensity of her problems as a kind of conveyer-belt to her husband but also, in the midst of climax after climax, was able to laugh over the foibles of the world swirling so rapidly around her.

I recall one day, lunching at the White House with members of the family, my amazement when the First Lady walked into the dining room clad in pants and sweater. "My mother-in-law detests these togs and I couldn't resist," she whispered to me, humanness out all over her.

My writing about Eleanor Roosevelt has to be scrappy and sporadic because that is the way this constantly expanding personality revealed itself not only to me but to the world.

I can never forget that, in the midst of a complicated and demanding world tour that amounted to a diplomatic mission, she found the compulsion and the time to write me a five page letter when my husband died.

And, then, I was present when the late Bernard Baruch paid her a visit and, while she sewed a loose button on his coat, he spent an hour discussing the nation's economy with her, her brain picking his for the facts which she continually stored away.

Later that same evening, she served hamburgers to a group from Boy's Town, Italy, and, the following morning, entertained a hundred youngsters from Wiltwyck School, one of her major interests, personally passing the frankfurters.

The admixture of physical and mental vitality which animated her must have been the force behind the compulsions to see, to do, to be, to care, and to spread her generosity in as many directions as possible. Take the night of Franklin D. Roosevelt's election to the first term of his presidency. Perhaps it was no more than a variation on the theme of many a presidential election, but it was my first close-up.

As early returns began to trickle into New York's Hotel Biltmore that election night, Mrs. Roosevelt tip-toed over to whisper to me, "Meet me at twelve o'clock in Louis Howe's office on the fourth floor. Be prepared to go home with me to Hyde Park for the final returns and to spend the night there."

In addition to Mrs. Roosevelt there were about twelve of us, including Steve Early, future secretary to the President, Frances Perkins, not yet Secretary of Labor, and Louis Howe, Franklin Roosevelt's confidant and political mentor, who took a late train to the lovely old manor house in Hyde Park presided over by Mrs. Sara Delano Roosevelt.

Our group gathered in the living room as car after car of Delanos and Roosevelts rolled up the driveway, while we sat tense, listening as the returns came pouring over the radio. About two o'clock in the morning Mrs. Roosevelt came into the room and whispered to me, "Franklin asked that you come into the room where he is."

In that room, surrounded by about a dozen men, sat the imminent President of the United States, who beckoned me to a vacant seat only once removed from him. Not a word was spoken, but the silence held to the last dramatic moment. When bedlam broke, there I sat at the President's right hand, a chance visitor happening in on history in the making.

It was four o'clock before we were scattered to our various lodgings. While I waited in a car for I knew not whom, Eleanor Roosevelt suddenly climbed in.

"Take Miss Hurst to the cottage, George," she said to

the chauffeur, "and then I will take over the car and drive to the airport."

"At four o'clock in the morning!" I exclaimed.

"Yes, Elliott is arriving. He's due about five-thirty. I'll just make it."

"I will go with you at this hour."

"No, you get your sleep. I have my knitting with me, in case of delay."

When I came out of my room for breakfast, Mrs. Roosevelt and Elliott were just arriving. She had waited two hours.

"There was a nice gentleman waiting for his daughter," she explained, "and he kept me company until he fell asleep, and I knitted on."

On another occasion I spent a week-end at the White House which began and ended on gale after gale of activities that had to do with affairs of state and protocol on down to the everyday problems of everyday people which occur in the White House even as they do in the smallest cottage in any American town.

I arrived from New York early morning to be met by a White House car. En route, we picked up Mrs. Roosevelt at a riding academy, following her early horseback ride. Arriving at the White House, I was instructed to report for breakfast at once. It was served in a small alcove off Mrs. Roosevelt's sitting room, a buffet affair. Mrs. Roosevelt was deep in stacked mail and mercilessly interrupted by telephone calls, secretaries, and housekeeper transactions.

Following breakfast, off we rushed to the Library of Congress for the sole purpose, mind you, of affording me the thrill of seeing my own books there. Five subsequent Eleanor Roosevelt appointments filled that morning: a visit to an orphanage, a talk before a women's club, a trip to a hospital to visit one of the Roosevelt boys recuperating from an appendicitis operation, a conference with Louis Howe, the purchase of an important gadget for the President's wheelchair.

At luncheon that same day there were only the President, daughter Anna Roosevelt, secretary Marguerite LeHand, Louis Howe, the First Lady and myself. I recall with some amusement that, when Mrs. Roosevelt hurried into the dining room, Anna affectionately adjusted her mother's blouse. "There is sometimes a hopeless discrepancy," she said smilingly, "between my mother and her clothes."

But luncheon was only a break in another average day in the life of this lady of the White House. Following a string of miscellaneous activities throughout the afternoon, we were back in time to change and rush off to dinner at the home of Henry Morgenthau Jr., then Secretary of the Treasury.

We returned to the White House about midnight in time to see a showing of a picture from a projector which Metro-Goldwyn-Mayer had newly installed for the President's private use. It was two o'clock when goodnights were finally said and I found myself alone in the Lincoln suite, but gone was my early morning resolve to remain awake instead of sleeping away the precious hours in a room hallowed by Abraham Lincoln. As I sat on the edge of the Lincoln bed, debating whether to retire without even removing my make-up, there came a knock at the door. I opened it to Mrs. Roosevelt in a bathing suit, pad and pencil in hand.

"What," she asked, pencil poised, "do you wish for breakfast?"

Then, entering the room, she tossed a towel to the floor.

"Remember, I was telling you about my Yoga exercises this morning?"

"This morning!" It seemed centuries back.

"I'll show you the standing on my head exercise." Suiting action to word, there she was straight as a monolith, feet in air!

Certainly the "humanness" alone of Eleanor Roosevelt does not add up to the ultimate grandeur of this woman through the years that were to call forth qualities that must have been inherent but might have gone unrealized. The Eleanor Roosevelt of a rather undistinguished girlhood and a wifehood which began under the domination of her mother-in-law scarcely presaged the opening of the folded wings within the heart and soul of this woman. Destiny leaned into her life and she took flight into world realms.

7

Albert Einstein

By WILLIAM L. LAURENCE

ALBERT EINSTEIN; born Ulm, Germany, March 14, 1879; son of middle-class Jewish parents; educated Munich, Milan, Aarau (Switzerland) and Federal Institute of Technology, Zurich; examiner Bern patent office, obtained doctorate University of Zurich, evolved theory of relativity, adjunct professor Zurich, professor German University of Prague, professor theoretical physics Federal Institute of Technology, professor of physics and director of theoretical physics Kaiser Wilhelm Institute in Berlin, fellow Institute for Advanced Study at Princeton; born German citizen, became Swiss citizen, resumed German citizenship in Berlin, deprived of German citizenship by Nazis, became American citizen; awarded Nobel Prize in Physics 1921; died Princeton, New Jersey, April 18, 1955.

William L. Laurence, born in Lithuania, came to the United States at the age of seventeen. A graduate of Harvard and Boston University Law School, he was led by his intense interest in science to become a science reporter and eventually science editor of the New York Times, *a post he held until his retirement in 1964. He was the only journalist present at the first test of the atomic bomb in New Mexico in 1945 and, as early as 1940, had written the first comprehensive accounts of the significance of the discovery of uranium fission. The official reporter of the atomic bomb missions over Hiroshima and Nagasaki, he is the winner of two Pulitzer prizes among many other awards and honors.*

STEIN SONG

There's a notable family called Stein:
There's Gertrude, there's Ep, and there's Ein.
Gert's writings are punk,
Ep's statues are junk,
And nobody understands Ein.
                              —Anonymous, c. 1930

ALBERT EINSTEIN was more than a hero of *our* time. He was a man of all time, of all ages.

In one simple mathematical formula—E=mc²—a miracle of intellectual creativity which summed up the knowledge of centuries, he showed man the way to the treasure house of the cosmos, the source of inexhaustible energy that could transform planet Earth into a paradise of plenty for all its inhabitants. Equally as important, he gave man a more profound understanding of his universe.

The scientific community the world over recognized him from the very beginning as the greatest of their fellowship. But more remarkable was the fact that mankind everywhere, who knew very little about science, looked upon him as a king among men.

To no other man in his lifetime had come the universal acclaim accorded to Albert Einstein. From his job as an unknown patent clerk in Bern, Switzerland, he streaked, meteor-like, across the intellectual firmament of his day and was at once recognized by the scientific élite as one of the giants in the history of human thought.

Einstein was only twenty-six when he published his

special theory of relativity, which revolutionized man's concepts of space and time, of matter, energy and light, and gave him an entirely new and much more profound understanding of his universe. He was thirty-six when he announced his general theory of relativity, which greatly expanded the scope of the special theory and provided a revolutionary concept of gravitation. But these were by no means the only great contributions to knowledge he made in those years.

Modern science rests on two major pillars. One is the theory of relativity, which deals with the cosmos at large. The second is the Quantum Theory, which deals with the constituents and forces within the atom. While Max Planck evolved the quantum theory, which revealed that radiant energy, instead of being continuous, comes in discrete units, or quanta, it was Einstein who developed Planck's original discovery into one of the fundamental pillars of modern science.

It was in 1905 that Einstein first published his paper on special relativity, a short article of thirty-one handwritten pages, entitled "Electrodynamics of Moving Bodies." That same year he published two other epoch-making papers. One provided the first explanation of the photoelectric effect (electronic or other electric effects produced by light), the principle underlying the photoelectric tube that made possible the long distance telephone, talking motion pictures, radio, television, computers and the Age of Automation. Another provided the first explanation of the phenomenon known as Brownian motion, which gave the best direct proof of the existence of the molecule and enabled man to observe accurately for the first time the motions of molecules and to determine their number in any given unit of volume.

Brownian motion is the irregular motion of small particles suspended in a liquid or a gas, which Einstein showed was caused by the bombardment of the particles by molecules of the medium. It was first observed by Robert Brown, the English botanist, in 1828. Einstein told me, however, that he had not learned of Brownian motion until after he had explained it, which is reminiscent of Daniel interpreting the dream of Nebuchadnezzar despite the king's inability to reveal to him what the dream was.

That simple Einstein formula (energy equals mass times the square of the speed of light) represented one of the boldest intellectual concepts in history. Until then, two of the basic laws of physics had been the law of conservation of matter and the law of conservation of energy, which meant that neither matter nor energy could be either created or destroyed, so that the total amount of matter or energy in the universe always remained the same. Not so, said Einstein. Matter and energy, instead of being two separate and distinct entities, are but one entity in two separate manifestations, matter being energy in the frozen state while energy was matter in the fluid state, just as ice is water in the frozen state while water was ice in the fluid form.

The formula revealed that any given amount of matter was the equivalent of a definite amount of energy. That was revolutionary enough, for it contradicted two of the fundamental laws of physics until then held to be inviolate. But most startling of all was the revelation, on translating the algebraic symbols of the formula, of the astronomical quantity of energy frozen in a minute amount of matter.

The formula states that the energy, in terms of ergs, frozen in one gram of matter equals the square of the velocity of light in terms of centimeters per second. Since the velocity of light is thirty billion centimeters per second, the formula reveals that one gram of any matter is the frozen equivalent of 900 billion billion ergs, or, in more familiar terms, of 25,000,000 kilowatt-hours. This is 18,000 million times the amount of energy liberated in the combustion of one gram of the best coal in pure oxygen. In explosive terms it is the equivalent of the energy liberated in the explosion of 20,000 tons of TNT.

First confirmation of the correctness of the formula was provided by the radioactive elements, radium and polonium, which, like the biblical burning bush, keep burning without being consumed. But the greatest proof of all, the most spectacular confirmation ever given to a purely intellectual concept, came on the morning of July 16, 1945, when the first atomic bomb exploded on the desert near Alamogordo, New Mexico, with a force equivalent of 20,000 tons of TNT, liberated from about one gram of the man-made element, plutonium. Three weeks later, when the atomic bomb exploded over Hiroshima and Nagasaki, it did more than bring the greatest war in history to a victorious end. What had been a pure idea that had exploded in the mind of one of the intellectual giants of history had materialized itself some forty years later into the greatest explosion seen until then on this planet and changed forever the lives of its inhabitants.

The explosion of the atomic bomb marked the first time on earth in which matter was converted into energy on a grand scale, exactly in accord with the Einstein formula, one gram, about two-fifths the weight of a dime, yielding an explosive force of 20,000 tons of TNT. By one of the bitter ironies of history, it was Einstein, one of the world's outstanding pacifists, who signed the historic letter to

United States President Franklin D. Roosevelt urging him to initiate the development of the atomic bomb, after it had been learned that the Nazis were working on one. But, after the war, he became one of the leaders in the movement to bring the bomb under international control.

In the entire course of man's recorded civilization, George Bernard Shaw said in an address introducing Einstein, only eight men—Pythagoras, Aristotle, Ptolemy, Copernicus, Galileo, Kepler, Newton and Einstein—succeeded in synthesizing the sum total of the knowledge of their day and age into a new vision of the universe, vaster than the one encompassed in the visions of their predecessors. He called these eight "Makers of the Universe."

"But," Shaw added, "even among these eight I must make a distinction. I have called them 'Makers of the Universe,' but some of them were only repairers. Only three of them made universes." He did not name the three, but it was obvious that he regarded Einstein as one of the three "makers of the universe." A second, undoubtedly, would be Newton. As for the third, my own choice would be Galileo, with Copernicus and Pythagoras as possible runner-ups, in the order named.

"Einstein's theory of relativity," wrote Bertrand Russell, one of the world's great mathematicians and philosophers, in 1924, "is probably the greatest synthetic achievement of the human intellect up to the present time. It sums up the mathematical and physical labors of more than 2,000 years. Pure geometry from Pythagoras to Riemann, the dynamics and astronomy of Galileo and Newton, the theory of electromagnetism as it resulted from the researches of Faraday, Maxwell and their successors, all are absorbed, with the necessary modifications, in the theories of Einstein."

The story of progress in pure and applied science has

been mainly the story of intellectual synthesis, the finding of new, formerly unsuspected relationships between seemingly unrelated phenomena. The synthesis by Michael Faraday of magnetism and electricity into a unified concept of electromagnetism led to his discovery of electromagnetic induction, the basic principle of the dynamo, which ushered in the Age of Electricity. James Clerk Maxwell's synthesis by pure mathematics of electromagnetism and light, revealing that light waves were electromagnetic in nature, led to his prediction of electromagnetic waves, discovered in 1888 by Heinrich Hertz, which ushered in the Age of Radio and Television and gave mankind powerful new tools for probing the mysteries of the universe. Lastly, Einstein's synthesis of matter and energy opened the way to the Atomic Age with its vast implications for the future of mankind.

Einstein dwelt all his life on a lonely scientific Sinai. Having achieved what Russell had described as "the greatest synthetic achievement of the human intellect," Einstein still found himself confronted with what was to him the profoundly disturbing fact that the universe, as revealed to him through relativity, appeared to flow in two seemingly parallel and independent streams, or "fields," the gravitational and electromagnetic fields, of which only the former could be traced directly to its source in the geometry of the world, the curvature of the four-dimensional space-time continuum. Convinced that both streams must have a common source in a larger cosmic geometrical design hidden from him, Einstein dedicated his life from 1916 until the end in 1955 to find the common origin of the two main cosmic streams.

What he was seeking with the consecrated devotion of a high priest for more than half his life was a simple set of logically coherent laws, expressed through aesthetically satisfying mathematical equations, that would unify the field of gravitation with the field of electromagnetism, a synthesis he called a "Unified Field Theory." In doing so he hoped to reduce the physical universe in its totality to a few simple fundamental concepts that would unify all its multifarious and seemingly unrelated manifestations into one all-embracing intellectual synthesis.

But the big prize at the end of the scientific rainbow kept eluding him like a will-o'-the-wisp and gradually led to his intellectual isolation from his fellows. He first believed he had achieved his goal in 1929, after thirteen years of concentrated effort, only to find it wanting on closer examination. In 1950 he thought he almost had it within his grasp, having overcome "all obstacles but one." In March 1953 he felt convinced that he had at last overcome that lone obstacle and thus had attained the crowning achievement of his life's work. Yet even then he ruefully admitted that he had "not yet found a practical way to confront the theory with experimental evidence," the crucial test for any theory.

What was even more serious, his "Unified Field Theory" did not properly account for the atom and its component particles (electrons, protons, neutrons, mesons, etc.) which appeared to be "singularities in the field," like flies in the cosmic "ointment." Despite these drawbacks, Einstein never wavered in his faith that the concept of the "pure field," free from "singularities" (namely, the particle concept of the atom and the atomic character, or quantum, of energy), was the only true approach to a well-ordered universe, and that eventually "the field" would fully account for the enfant terrible of the cosmos—the atom and its nucleus and the vast forces within it.

Behind the Einstein quest for a Unified Field Theory—actually a quest to find a uniform set of cosmic laws for the universe of the stars and galaxies and the universe of the atom, of which the stars and galaxies are constituted—lay one of the greatest intellectual schisms in the history of human thought, involving fundamental questions that had divided philosophers throughout the ages: monism versus dualism; continuity versus discontinuity; causality versus chance; free will versus determinism.

Einstein believed that the physical universe was one continuous field, governed by one logical set of laws, in which every individual event is inexorably determined by immutable laws of causality. On the other hand, the vast majority of modern-day physicists champion the quantum theory, which decrees a discontinuous universe of discrete particles and quanta (atoms) of energy, in which probability takes the place of causality and determinism is supplanted by chance.

Whereas Einstein sought for unity, the quantum theory, of which Einstein was one of the principal founders, regards the physical universe as dual in nature, everything in it manifesting itself as both particle and wave. The theory has as one of its keystones the Heisenberg uncertainty principle, according to which it is impossible to predict individual events, so that all knowledge is based on probability and is thus at best only statistical in nature. The uncertainty principle has, furthermore, led present-day physicists (with the exception of Einstein) to follow the doctrine that there is no causality or determinism in nature, events, as far as human knowledge goes, taking place purely by chance.

Einstein alone stood in majestic solitude against what he regarded as the heresies of the quantum theory. Granting that it had had brilliant successes in solving many of the mysteries of the atom and the complex behavior and inter- actions of radiation, phenomena that no other theory had succeeded in explaining, Einstein nevertheless insisted that a theory of discontinuity and uncertainty, of duality and of chance, was an "incomplete theory," that eventually uni- versal laws would be found establishing a continuous, unitary universe, governed by immutable laws of cause and effect in which all individual events were predictable.

"I cannot believe that the good Lord shoots craps!" he said. His scientific credo is expressed in the inscription on the marble fireplace in the mathematics building of the Institute for Advanced Study, at Princeton, New Jersey. It reads, in German: "Cunning the good Lord is, but mali- cious He is not!" which means that God is not maliciously playing tricks on us but is only challenging us to gain understanding of the subtleties of His universe.

As the years passed, the figure of Einstein the man be- came more and more remote, while that of Einstein the legend came ever nearer to the masses of mankind. They grew to know him not as a universe-maker whose theories they could not hope to understand, but as a world citizen, an outstanding spiritual leader of his generation, a symbol of the human spirit and its noblest aspirations.

As Dr. Philipp Frank, Einstein's biographer, wrote in 1947:

"The world around Einstein has changed very much since he published his first discoveries . . . but his atti- tude to the world around him has not changed. He has remained an individualist who prefers to be unencum- bered by social relations, and at the same time a fighter for social equality and human fraternity.

"Many famous scholars live in the distinguished university town, but no inhabitant will simply number Einstein as one among many other famous people. For the people of Princeton in particular, and for the world at large, he is not just a great scholar, but rather one of the legendary figures of the twentieth century. Einstein's acts and words are not simply noted and judged as facts; instead each has its symbolic significance."

"Saintly," "noble," and "lovable," were the words used to describe him by those who knew him even casually. He radiated humor, warmth and kindliness. He loved jokes and laughed easily.

He was always patient and humorous in his answers to the inevitable request to explain relativity in simple terms. The first such occasion was his answer given to reporters on his first visit to New York in April, 1921.

"It is a theory of space and time," he said.

"Oh, come on, Professor, we need a little more than that," the reporters persisted.

"Well," said Einstein, "just as a joke and not to be taken too literally, relativity has this effect on any thought of the universe; up to now the conceptions of time and space have been such that if everything in the universe were taken away, if there was nothing left, then there would still remain to man time and space. But under my theory, even time and space would cease to exist because they are inseparably bound up with the conceptions of matter."

This satisfied the reporters. "Einstein said today that he had destroyed time and space."

A still simpler explanation was provided by Einstein to his secretary, who was much annoyed by visitors asking her to tell them what relativity really meant. He directed her to give the following answer:

"When a young man spends two hours with a pretty girl, it seems like a minute. But if the young man were to sit on a hot stove for but a fraction of a second it would seem to him like two hours. That's relativity!"

Princeton residents would see him walk in their midst, a familiar figure yet a stranger, a close neighbor yet at the same time a visitor from another world. And as he grew older, his otherworldliness became more pronounced, yet his human warmth did not diminish.

He loved children, being himself childlike. Despite the great demands made upon him, he still found time to help a little girl with her arithmetic, as one surprised Princeton mother found out after her young daughter failed to return from school one afternoon. On being asked where she had been, the child explained that she had been having trouble with her arithmetic and had called upon Professor Einstein for help.

"He invited me in," the child said, "gave me crackers and milk, and explained my arithmetic lesson to me much better than my teacher. He told me to come back again any time I needed help in my lessons."

When the alarmed mother called on Einstein to apologize, Einstein told her she had nothing to apologize for.

"I have certainly learned more from your child than she did from me," he assured her.

There is also the story of the Christmas Eve of his first year at Princeton. A group of children sang carols outside his house on Mercer Street, and when they had finished they rang his doorbell and informed him that they were collecting money to buy Christmas presents for the poor. Telling them to wait, Einstein soon re-appeared with his violin and accompanied them in their singing.

While it is generally believed that he was a virtuoso on the violin, this was far from the view of professional musicians. Once he played his fiddle and was accompanied on the piano by Leopold Godowsky, famous pianist, composer and teacher. Suddenly, Mr. Godowsky turned around and addressed the great man in the manner of a teacher admonishing an inept pupil.

"Hey, Professor," he shouted, "can't you count? One, two, three, four!"

Outward appearances meant nothing to Einstein. Princetonians, old and young, soon got used to the long-haired figure in pullover sweater and unpressed slacks wandering in their midst, a knitted stocking cap covering his head in winter.

"My passionate interest in social justice and social responsibility," he wrote, "has always stood in curious contrast to a marked lack of desire for direct association with men and women. I am a horse for single harness, not cut out for tandem or team work. I have never belonged wholeheartedly to country or state, to my circle of friends, or even to my own family. These ties have always been accompanied by a vague aloofness, and the wish to withdraw into myself increases with the years.

"Such isolation is sometimes bitter, but I do not regret being cut off from the understanding and sympathy of other men. I lose something by it, to be sure, but I am compensated for it in being rendered independent of the customs, opinions and prejudices of others, and am not tempted to rest my peace of mind upon such shiftless foundations."

It was this independence that made Einstein at times the center of controversy, mainly because of his championship of highly unpopular causes. He declared himself a staunch pacifist in Germany during World War I and brought down upon his head a storm of violent criticism from all sides. When, following the German invasion of Belgium in violation of treaty, outstanding representatives of German art and science signed the "Manifesto of Ninety-two German Intellectuals" asserting that German culture and German militarism were identical, Einstein refused to sign and again faced ostracism and the wrath of the multitude.

But he never wavered when his conscience dictated that he take a course of action, no matter how unpopular.

He was a severe critic of modern methods of education. "It is nothing short of a miracle," he said, "that modern methods of instruction have not yet entirely strangled the holy curiosity of inquiry. For this delicate little plant, aside from stimulation, stands mainly in need of freedom."

His political ideal, he emphasized frequently, was democracy. "The distinctions separating the social classes," he wrote, "are false. In the last analysis they rest on force. I am convinced that degeneracy follows every autocratic system of violence, for violence inevitably attracts moral inferiors. . . . For this reason I have always been passionately opposed to such regimes as exist in Russia and Italy today." This was written in 1931, two years before Hitler came to power.

His love for the oppressed also led him to become a strong supporter of Zionism. In November, 1952, following the death of Chaim Weizmann, Israel's first president, Einstein was asked if he would accept the post as Weizmann's successor. He replied that he was deeply touched by the offer but that he was not qualified for the job. He never undertook functions, he said, he could not fulfill to his own satisfaction.

After August, 1945, following the dropping of the atomic bomb over Hiroshima and Nagasaki, Einstein devoted much of his time in an attempt to arouse the world's consciousness to the bomb's dangers. He became the chairman of the Emergency Committee of Atomic Scientists, organized to make the people of the world aware of the potential horrors of atomic warfare and the necessity for the international control of atomic energy. He believed that real peace could be achieved only by total disarmament and the establishment of a "restricted world government," a "supranational judicial and executive body empowered to decide questions of immediate concern to the security of the nations."

Explaining his great love for music, he said: "In my life, the artistically visionary plays no mean role. After all, the work of a research scientist germinates upon the soil of imagination, of vision. Just as the artist arrives at his conceptions partly by intuition, so a scientist must also have a certain amount of intuition."

"Ideas come from God," he once said to a fellow scientist.

While he did not belong to a formal, dogmatic religion, Einstein was a deeply religious man. He referred to it as the "cosmic religion," which he defined as a seeking on the part of the individual who feels it "to experience the totality of existence as a unity full of significance."

"I assert," he wrote, "that the cosmic religious experience is the strongest and the noblest driving force behind scientific research. No one who does not appreciate the terrific exertions and, above all, the devotion, without which pioneer creation in scientific thought cannot come into being, can judge the strength of the feeling out of which alone such work, turned away as it is from immediate, practical life, can grow . . .

"The most beautiful and profound emotion we can experience is the mystical. It is the source of all true art and science. He to whom the emotion is a stranger, who can no longer pause to wonder and stand rapt in awe, is as good as dead; his eyes are closed. This insight into the mystery of life, coupled though it be with fear, also has given rise to religion. To know that what is impenetrable to us really exists, manifesting itself as the highest wisdom and the most radiant beauty which our dull faculties can comprehend only in their primitive forms—this knowledge, this feeling, is at the center of true religiousness. In this sense, and in this sense only, I belong to the ranks of devoutly religious men.

"I cannot imagine a God who rewards and punishes the objects of His Creation, whose purposes are modeled after our own—a God, in short, who is but a reflection of human frailty. Neither can I believe that the individual survives the death of his body, although feeble souls harbor such thoughts through fear or ridiculous egotism. It is enough for me to contemplate the mystery of conscious life perpetuating itself through all eternity, to reflect upon the marvelous structure of the universe which we can dimly perceive, and to try humbly to comprehend even an infinitesimal part of the intelligence manifested in nature.

"My religion consists of humble admiration of the illimitable Superior Spirit who reveals Himself in the slight details we are able to perceive with our frail and feeble minds. That deeply emotional conviction of the presence of a superior reasoning power, which is revealed in the incomprehensible universe, forms my idea of God."

"The most incomprehensible thing about the world," he said, "is that it is comprehensible."

In a lighter vein, Einstein told an audience at the Sorbonne, in Paris: "If my theory of relativity is proven successful, Germany will claim me as a German and France will declare that I am a citizen of the world. Should my theory prove untrue, France will say that I am a German, while Germany will declare that I am a Jew."

In 1921, when Einstein made his first visit to the United

States, interest in his theory and its meaning was so great that Representative J. J. Kindred of New York requested the Speaker of the House for permission to insert a popular presentation of relativity into the Congressional Record.

Representative (later Senator) David I. Walsh of Massachusetts asked: "Does the gentleman from New York expect to get the subject in such shape that we can understand the theory?"

Mr. Kindred replied: "I have been earnestly busy with this theory for three weeks and am beginning to see some light."

"What legislation will it bear upon?" Mr. Walsh persisted.

To which Mr. Kindred replied: "It may bear upon the legislation of the future as to general relations with the cosmos."

It was at about this time that an American hostess asked the visiting scientist to explain relativity "in a few simple words."

"Madam," said Einstein, "a blind man was walking with a friend down a hot and dusty road. His friend said: 'Oh, for a nice drink of milk!' 'Drink I know,' said the blind man, 'but what is this milk?' 'A white liquid.' 'Liquid I know, but what is white?' 'The color of a swan's feathers.' 'Feathers I know, but what is a swan?' 'A bird with a crooked neck.' 'Neck I know, but what is crooked?' Whereupon the friend lost patience. He seized the blind man's arm and straightened it. 'That is straight,' he said. Then, bending it at the elbow, 'and this is crooked.' 'Ah,' cried the blind man, 'now I understand what you mean by milk!' "

8

Pope John XXIII

By BARRETT McGURN

ANGELO GIUSEPPE RONCALLI; born Sotto il Monte, near Bergamo, Italy, November 25, 1881; son of tenant farmer; ordained priest, secretary to Bishop of Bergamo, soldier and later chaplain World War I, assigned Society for the Propagation of the Faith in Rome, archbishop and apostolic visitor in Bulgaria, nuncio and apostolic delegate to Turkey and Greece, nuncio France after World War II, cardinal and patriarch of Venice, elected pope October 28, 1958, succeeding Pius XII, took name John XXIII, wrote encyclical *Mater et Magister* and convened Second Vatican Council in Rome; died Vatican, June 3, 1963; succeeded by Paul VI.

Barrett McGurn, then Rome correspondent of the New York Herald Tribune, *served his two terms as president of the Stampa Estera, the foreign correspondents' club in Rome, during the reign of Pope John XXIII. He is in the unique position of also having been president of the Overseas Press Club in New York for two terms. As a correspondent for the Army weekly* Yank *during World War II, he won a Purple Heart on Bougainville. After the war, he served as* Herald Tribune *bureau chief in Rome, Moscow and Paris and won the OPC's annual award for best foreign correspondence for his reporting of the 1956 Hungarian rev-*

olution. The author of a number of books, he is now the
United States press attaché in Rome.

JOHN XXIII, the 260th of the popes of Catholic history, was
not an exceptional intellectual nor a great theologian. He
had been a poor student in grade school in the late 1900s
in the northern Italian Alpine foothills. At sixty, the
retirement age for many, the future pope was an obscure
cleric known to but a few Italian countrymen. Yet Pope
John had a more profound influence on religious history
than all but a handful in four hundred years.

I will never forget one meeting with Pope John. I had co-
authored a series of articles about the pontiff in the New
York *Herald Tribune.* The *Reader's Digest* bought con-
densation rights and the piece was reproduced in a
dozen *Digest* editions. Pope John granted an audience, at
which I gave him a white leather-bound album with clippings of the story as it had appeared around the world.

The pope was a short, plump man, barrel-shaped. His
face was round, his nose large, a triple chin bulging beneath a wide smiling mouth. With a white beard, a rud-
dier complexion, and a red suit instead of a white cassock,
John could have posed for everyone's idea of Santa Claus.
Certainly he had the jolly kindness of Father Christmas.

We met in one of the ornate brocade-walled side rooms
of the papal apartments in the centuries-old Vatican palace. A monsignor fidgeted at the pontiff's elbow, anxious
that I be done with my interview so that the pope might
move on to the endless masses of others awaiting their own
brief contact with the holy man. Popes see an average of
500,000 persons a year, some in small personal meetings
such as mine, many in immense throngs inside St. Peter's

Basilica. With all the demands on the pontiff's time there are never enough moments for all.

I flipped through the pages of the book, showing the old gentleman how you say "good Pope John" in Finnish, Swedish, French, German, Portuguese and Spanish, and how local editions handled the article in South Africa, India, Canada and other places around the globe. There was a subtly austere tone in Spain, a more relaxed but no less admiring approach in the Anglo-Saxon areas. Headlines and picture captions made the difference.

"This publication has a circulation of 25 million and, in all, about 100 million readers, the largest circulation in the world," I told the prelate. He nodded with amusement.

"Hold on to this," he said to the fussing monsignor beside him. "I'll take a better look at it later."

Popes are supposed to fit a pattern, like kings and admirals, movie stars and "big businessmen." In the case of popes it is assumed that they are too busy with Church documents, appointments of the Catholic bishops of the world, and ecclesiastical ceremonies to interest themselves even in such vast personal publicity as a *Reader's Digest* story represents. But if others in the papacy and elsewhere attempt to live their popularly assigned part, John was different. He was his simple, honest self and for that he offered no apologies.

I stepped back to free the pope for his next audience but he reached a hand to detain me.

"Here is a thought for you," and he looked me in the eye. "You are a reporter. If on the last day of your life you can say that you have always been a servant of what is true, you will be able to die happily."

Pope John was eighty then, and death was often on his mind. He spoke of it frequently, especially in his first weeks as pontiff. The rumor in Rome was that Pope John had been elected because he was a cardinal, an Italian, a veteran of the Vatican diplomatic service, a world traveler of some limited accomplishments, a former worker inside the Holy See headquarters, a local bishop in charge of an area and, most important, an old man.

The pope was elected at 78. Pius XII, a devout but authoritarian man, had ruled the Catholic Church for nineteen years and had imposed a personal and austere stamp on the world headquarters of the Catholic Church and, indeed, on the faith itself. Those of us who were in Rome covering it for the world press understood, thanks to our "highly placed sources" and to our own most astute imaginings, that the fifty cardinals wanted extra time in which to decide upon Pius XII's "real" successor. The best way to gain time was to select someone so far along in years that he could not survive in the pontificate for very long.

Some of the old popes of history lived for a year or two, Pope John told many of his early audiences, "I hope I have as long!"

As it turned out, Pope John lived four years as the spiritual leader of the world's 500 million Roman Catholics, as the world's most important single spokesman for moral, spiritual and religious values. Those four years deeply and irreversibly changed the globe's greatest Christian faith (the Catholics compose five-ninths of the Christians of the world).

The essence of Pope John's revolution was to "open windows," as he reportedly phrased it, on a world born since the Middle Ages, since the four-century-old Protestant Reformation, since the industrial revolution, and since the beginning of the space age. With a calm fiat, the pope brushed aside centuries of hostility toward Protestants, set a reform of the severe Holy Office (once the Inquisition) in motion, and opened doors to ecumenical and rationalist scholarship which the Index (the list of forbidden books) had barred for generations.

Few literary pretensions were reflected in Pope John's library when he was cardinal-patriarch of Venice before his election to the papacy. There were guidebooks aplenty, a souvenir of years of sightseeing while on missions as a Vatican diplomat in Bulgaria, Turkey, Greece, North Africa and France. Books of modern literature, sociology and theology were few. Yet writers had a special place in the aged man's heart.

I had occasion to observe that on a second visit to Pope John. This time another publication, the *Catholic Digest*, had asked me to give the churchman two bound volumes of their 25th anniversary editions. I had written some pieces for them, so I agreed. This time Pope John thought of me as a "Catholic writer" so his appropriate concise personal message was tailored differently from what he had said at our previous meeting.

"You are a writer," he remarked. "Keep this in mind. Writing, too, like the work of the clergy itself, is a form of apostolate."

Writers, in short, need not think of themselves as uninvolved observers of aimless mankind. They, too, could feel rightly that they carried the flag of a mission.

People streamed past in front of the old pope, and it is certain that he did not always understand who was who. United States Secretary of the Treasury Douglas Dillon, then famous as the man with his name on the American dollar bill, was introduced in one audience. The pontiff caught just the word "secretary."

"Ah, a secretary," he said, apparently assuming that Mr.

Dillon was one of the lesser members of the group before him. "Yes, secretaries, too, have an important job to do!"

The incident reflected a certain amount of confusion, understandable in a near-octogenarian catapulted into one of the planet's most public positions. But it also underlined the gently affectionate way in which the unpretending pope reached out to embrace all as brothers, cabinet members and the humblest "secretaries" alike.

In three decades of reporting on Catholic Church and Vatican affairs for one of the world's great papers (the lamented *Herald Tribune*), I had not heard of Angelo Roncalli until two months before he became "Pope John." I was not alone in my ignorance. The late Francis Cardinal Spellman of New York, who was the most famous member of the College of Cardinals, asked an American diplomat after John's election: "Who is he? You served with him when he was a nuncio. What can you tell me about him?"

Angelo Roncalli, after an inauspicious start as a mountain schoolboy (undernourishment and exhausting walks to and from class may have explained early indolence), began to study seriously in his early teens. The change occurred just in time. A parish priest sponsored additional studies and Angelo entered the local seminary. He did well enough there to be given final instruction in Rome, the treatment reserved for those who have aroused the greatest expectations. In Rome, by coincidence, a prominent Vatican cleric, Archbishop Radini-Tedeschi, was transferred to the Roncalli home area as bishop. He needed a secretary. Newly ordained Father Roncalli, the only candidate at hand, was given the assignment. Within a few years the well-introduced bishop had made his young assistant known to a generation of North Italian church leaders, one of whom, Monsignor Achilles Ratti, became pope (Pius

XI, 1922–1939). Those introductions guaranteed that the unknown farmboy would be remembered.

Pius XI, not long after his coronation, sent Monsignor Roncalli to Bulgaria as a papal diplomat. It was an appropriate assignment for a stolid, amiable type: little to do but to chat with Orthodox prelates after 1,000 years of Catholic-Orthodox separation, in the hope that on some distant day Christian unity might be recovered. No one expected to live to see Church reunion but then no one foresaw the stocky Monsignor Roncalli eventually on Peter's throne.

In 1944, Pius XII (the pope of 1939–1958) required someone as nuncio to France, Vatican diplomacy's number one post. It had to be a prelate who had been in no way involved with Hitler's occupation of Europe. General Charles de Gaulle would not listen to any argument that the churchmen had been unarmed victims of military circumstance, compelled by the nature of things to carry on religiously under the heels of an uninvited occupier.

By the same token, to pick up the pieces in war-shattered France, the ideal nuncio had to be one who had not, as the Francis Spellmans had, borne aloft the banner of the conquering democracies. What was needed was a bland edgeless peacemaker, a man without enemies.

"You must be crazy to think of me," Nuncio Roncalli told the papal Substitute Secretary of State, Monsignor Domenico Tardini, who later related some of his experiences to a group of us at the Rome foreign press club.

"You can be sure it wasn't I who suggested you," the frank Tardini retorted. "Only one person spoke of you: the pope."

Pius XII and John XXIII were very diverse personalities. Pius XII, though himself an Italian, seemed to worry about such elements of the Italian character as the reputation for chronic tardiness. He put punctuality high on the list of the many virtues he strove to practice.

"I wanted to tell you that I was the one who had the idea about you, but I am sorry that I will be able to give you only ten minutes now," Pius XII is said to have told his new nuncio.

"All I need to know is that you want me," Pius XII's future successor is reported to have answered. "I can make you a gift of the remaining eight minutes."

Whatever may be true about the story, there is no doubt that Pope John, on Peter's chair, put punctuality well down his own list of priorities.

"My husband was never treated so badly in his life," one ambitious wife of an American senator fumed after one of Pope John's audiences. "We were there a bit ahead of time, naturally, but then we had to wait for an hour! And we were in and out in five minutes!"

The senator, no doubt, had his local "Catholic vote" in mind. But the two men somehow did not hit it off. There was the usual pressure of more visitors waiting in line. John's easy-going manner boomeranged this time. One can presume, however, that a long list of delighted persons who used up bits of the senator's assigned period had left, as most of John's visitors did, with a lift in their hearts.

John was among the least likely papal candidates until the logic of "an old Italian bishop and cardinal with Vatican and world experience" began to guide the minds of the cardinal voters.

"I can't tell you who will be pope," said one who had known Nuncio Roncalli in France, "but I can tell you one cardinal out of fifty whom it will *not* be. That one is Cardinal Roncalli. I had lunch with him three times a month for years and I can assure you he possesses nothing but small talk."

He was not, in short, a man for great sociological, ideological or theological pronouncements. There was more than a half truth in the observation, but what the nuncio's friend had missed was a manly common sense and affection which could work miracles of good will when cold reasoning could not. The ability beneath the charm had been hinted soon after Nuncio Roncalli's arrival in France.

"Here's a list of thirty-three bishops for you to fire as Nazi collaborators," General De Gaulle, in effect, told the papal emissary.

A great many of the prelates had been more interested in prayers than in politics, the new nuncio was sure. A recovering forgiving Europe on some tomorrow probably would be less harsh in berating churchmen who had failed to do more for the Resistance. The nuncio stalled for time.

"Give me the detailed charges on each," he requested.

Paper work! Investigations! And at a time when there was so much else to do!

It ended with the removal of three of the thirty-three. One of the thirty whom the nuncio saved went on to become one of France's, and De Gaulle's, most popular post-war cardinals.

I was present in St. Peter's Square when John XXIII walked out on the basilica balcony for his first contact as pope with the outer world. The impression of all around me was negative. After nineteen years of the reign of the gaunt Pius XII, everyone had the idea that a pope should be slim.

"*Ma è un porco!* He's a real porker!" our seven-year-old

daughter, Betsy, shocked us by commenting at home later that evening.

Betsy, a natural linguist and mimic, had been at the local soda parlor when the television ran live coverage of the balcony scene. What Betsy remarked at home was nothing more than the frank gasp and saucy judgment she had heard from the tart-tongued Romans around the same TV set. Romans have seen popes come and go for twenty centuries and, like Missourians, have to be shown.

Within an instant of those first observations about the new pope's rotundity, a second impression took root. With no nonsense, the new pontiff stepped to the balcony's railing and, in a fatherly voice, begged a blessing. He waved to us, turned away, and ordered all the cardinals to return to the conclave for a final night and supper together. An hour before he had been one among many in the gathering of the cardinals. Already he was their director though still, at table, their brother.

"Cardinals advise, but it's the pope who makes decisions," the new pontiff, with gentle firmness, told Cardinal Spellman in my presence. The cardinal had insisted that Americans were carrying a heavy tax and military burden in helping the world's hundreds of millions of needy, but the pope persisted in appealing for even more foreign aid. A month earlier there had been no doubt which of the two clerics was the more illustrious. Now it was John's duty to lead according to his own lights. Unhesitatingly, he did.

Covering Pope John was a fulltime assignment for Rome reporters in the weeks after the churchman's elevation. News, as the *Times* of London once said, is "the record of change." It seemed for a while as if John would change everything. He invited guests for dinner; the rule had been that popes sup alone.

One report was that John interrupted an audience to say to a visitor: "I'm having tea. Will you join me?"

The tourists' lookout atop the Michelangelo dome above St. Peter's was always closed from four to five P.M. for Pius XII's daily walks in the Vatican gardens. "Let them in; I won't do anything down there to scandalize them," John is said to have remarked as he revoked the injunction.

Famous callers inhibited the new pope no more than did newsmen. When President Eisenhower came on a visit, photographers got a shot of the pope and the president chuckling.

"What was the joke?" the *Herald Tribune* queried me.

"It was a remark of the pope's," the interpreter told me. "He had been chatting in Italian as I translated. Then he unfolded a speech in English and, as he started to struggle with it, he told the President, "Now you'll hear *di bello!* Now you'll hear a beaut!"

John knew that his English limped. He did his best in all directions and, good-humoredly, had no apologies beyond that.

A former colleague of the diplomatic corps sent word to the new pope that he would love to see him again.

"Well, they won't let me go over to your hotel," John responded. "But I'd be glad to receive you if you'd come over here."

The audience was arranged and the pope gave his old associate a Vatican knighthood.

The pope helped change the name of the official American ambassadorial residence in Rome.

"How's Villa La Pariola these days?" Pope John asked American Ambassador Frederick L. Reinhardt. "I remember sixty years ago when it was the summer recreational ground for the Rome seminary. I used to walk there on Sundays."

The name of the residence in 1960 when the two talked was Villa Taverna, which had been its designation since 1920, when the Taverna family had bought it. Mr. Reinhardt had seen the "Villa La Pariola" name on an old deed so he was not caught flat-footed. He picked up the conversational gambit, and he did not forget the exchange. A few months later he restored the villa's historical appellation, La Pariola. The residence is so known today and, presumably, henceforth will be called by the name Pope John accidentally revived.

Pope John's willingness to review and revise traditions encouraged me, while president of the foreign correspondents' association of Italy (*Stampa Estera*) to invite him and his cardinal for interfaith reunion, Augustine Bea, for meals at our club. Cardinal Bea replied first, "I'll have to get permission higher up."

A monsignor told me later what happened when my invitation, relayed by the cardinal, reached Pope John.

"Agree!" the monsignor urged. "It will be a good thing to have a friendly contact with the newsmen."

The pope threw up his hands.

"Why not?" he said.

"Why not" was because it had not been done before. For the innocently daring Pope John, a negative reason was no reason at all.

The cardinal came for lunch and was a winningly informative guest. Then came time for an answer to the second invitation, the one to the pope himself.

"No," was the reply. "But come over to the Vatican and I'll give you all a good audience. If you, as the president, want to make a speech, fine, I'll listen to it."

That, too, was unheard of. With the help of Robert Mengin and Max Bergerre of Agence France Presse I wrote a three-minute talk in French saying all I wanted to get across. My main point was:

"Happy birthday. [It was John's eightieth anniversary.] Please take a look at Vatican press relations; they can stand improvement."

As the Vatican had requested, I had sent a copy of the speech ahead of time so the pope's aides in the Secretariate of State could draw up a response.

The pope gave us an hour, three times as long as the usual audience for kings and presidents.

"When he is finished, say 'won't you add a few words,' " the pope's private secretary, Monsignor Loris Capovilla, advised me as we assembled inside the gilded Vatican throne room.

I was taken aback. It was enough to ask the pope for a speech, and he had a fifteen-minute address in French ready for us. It was more than enough to be allowed to say a few words of our own. To end such an encounter like Oliver Twist by asking for more was something which I, as the representative of the world press in Italy, would never have dreamed of doing had the pope's own right hand man not advocated it. I assumed that the monsignor was talking in John's own name so, risking the wrath of my protocol-minded colleagues, I rose at the end and said in Italian, "Can you say a few more words?"

That was what Pope John needed. He put down the stiff prepared text which had promised better press contacts (a promise amply fulfilled later on). He grinned. We re-called that his French was fluent, but it was nonetheless an uncomfortable second language. In his own Italian, he said:

"O, you newsmen! I'll never forget my own first by-line. It was in our diocesan newspaper, and I had just been ordained. . . ."

For twenty more minutes, the pontiff reminisced and joked. Many a cold newshawk heart melted.

The central work of Pope John was to break down barriers separating those who worship the same God by different names, and to encourage all to live easily and immediately with a God sometimes lost behind formalisms.

An example was a visit by the head of the Scottish Presbyterian church.

"You don't have cardinals," the pope told his "low church" caller. "Well, you don't need them the way I do. I'm elected for life. I need cardinals as advisers. But your term is only for two years!"

The visitor went away charmed.

In what he called "a moment's inspiration," Pope John summoned an ecumenical council, a law-making assembly of the Catholic bishops for a review and updating of the Church, the first such overhaul in the four centuries since the beginning of Protestantism. Some in the papal entourage feared bitter debate and confusion. A half-concealed effort was made to reverse the pope's decision. But John insisted. The council met from 1962 to 1965, and had sweeping effects of modernization which only now are being experienced fully and beneficently.

Early in 1962 Pope John was found to have cancer. As the world mourned, he died slowly, hoping to survive until the Vatican council he had called finished its task.

"Never mind," he told aides. "I'm not afraid. My bags are packed! The Lord can take me anytime."

He died in 1963. A half decade later, Pope John souvenirs still are among the most popular papal mementos in Rome. The cult of popes rarely outlives them but, in John's case, if anything, the devotion grows. Modernists and traditionalists revere the memory of this holy peasant. The slow machinery of a canonization is grinding. Not many years hence the pope of "why not," the nuncio who was passed over by all but Pius XII in the 1944 hunt for a Paris nuncio, the one cardinal of 1958 who "definitely could not be considered for pope," is likely to be called by a new name once again, this time Saint John XXIII.

9

Albert Schweitzer

By NORMAN COUSINS

ALBERT SCHWEITZER; born Kayserberg, Alsace, France, January 14, 1875; son of Lutheran minister; educated local schools Günsbach and Münster, studied organ music in Paris with Charles Marie Widor, studied theology and philosophy Universities of Strasbourg, Paris (Sorbonne) and Berlin; successively preacher Strasbourg, principal of Strasbourg theological college, author authoritative biography of Johann Sebastian Bach and *The Quest of the Historical Jesus*; at age of thirty decided to become medical missionary and obtained medical degree at Strasbourg, sailed for Gabon in French Equatorial Africa to set up native hospital at Lambaréné; interned as enemy alien during World War I, continued to write on theology and philosophy and to give lectures and organ concerts in Europe to support work at Lambaréné; awarded Goethe Prize of Frankfurt, Germany, in 1928 and Nobel Peace Prize in 1952; died Lambaréné, September 4, 1965.

Norman Cousins is now editor of Saturday Review, *chairman of the editorial committee of* McCall's *and a director of the McCall Corporation. He has written many books, including* Dr. Schweitzer of Lambaréné, *and is a recipient of the Overseas Press Club annual award for the best interpre-*

*tation of foreign affairs in a magazine and some fifteen
other writing awards. He is President of the World Association of World Federalists and Chairman of Hiroshima
Peace Center Associates.*

ALBERT SCHWEITZER's Hospital at Lambaréné, in Gabon,
Africa, is around a bend in the river and you do not have a
good view of it until you swing around and come toward it
downstream. In order to do this your canoe continues perhaps a third of a mile or more on the opposite shore beyond the Hospital so that when you cross the river the
current will not carry you beyond the dock.

The first time I went to see Dr. Schweitzer in Lambaréné
was in January 1958. As the canoe swung into midstream, I
discovered some figures dressed in white walking down the
hill from the Hospital toward the small dock. When we
were about three hundred feet from the dock, I recognized
the Doctor. He was at the edge of the dock now, waving to
us. Then, when the canoe was within perhaps fifty feet, he
began to call out directions. It was like a ferry being eased
into her slip by commands from the bridge.

"*À gauche! À gauche!* (Left! To the left!) " the Doctor
cried out. *Lentement!* (Slowly!) "

Then sharply,

"*Arrêtez!* (Stop!) "

He stooped and grabbed the prow, then eased the canoe
alongside the dock. The Africans held the pirogue firm,
and the Doctor reached over to help us out, one at a time.
As he took my arm, he introduced himself.

The Doctor then escorted me up the hill to the Hospital.
The lane was narrow and we threaded our way past some
small shacks and enclosures on the hillside. The ground

underneath was moist and slippery and had the consistency
of a chicken-yard. The reason was readily apparent. Almost
everywhere I looked there were chickens, ducks, goats.
Then the path opened out on a courtyard with low-lying
wooden structures. The building on the left was mounted
on concrete piles about six or seven feet above the ground.
This was where the Doctor and the immediate members of
his staff lived. Directly opposite were some utility and stor-
age buildings, also set on concrete piles a few feet off the
ground.

At the foot of the steps leading to the Doctor's quarters
was Mrs. Schweitzer. I had been told she was not well and
was able to get about the hospital grounds only with the
greatest difficulty. The Doctor introduced me. Mrs.
Schweitzer spoke in English; she was most gracious, apolo-
gizing for the fact that she was unable to accompany me to
my room, and saying she hoped I would drop by for a chat
after I got settled. We resumed our walk, the Doctor
leading the way past several other frame buildings, each
with its dark-red corrugated iron rooftop. One could
hardly see the sky because of the thick benevolent over-
head shelter from the trees.

As we walked along, I began to see why some visitors to
Lambaréné came away with negative impressions. The
word "hospital" summons up images of immaculate cor-
ridors, white sheets, total sanitation. These notions were
badly jolted when one saw the Hospital at Lambaréné for
the first time. Countless numbers of goats and chickens
wandered at will all over the place; even when they were
not in sight their presence was perceptible. Hanging heavily in the dank air was the smoke from the dozens of crude
burners used by the Africans for their cooking. There was

also an inexplicably sweet and somewhat sticky smell—perhaps from the cooking or from fallen and fermented fruit.

The sanitary facilities were at an absolute minimum. There were only two outhouses, one for each sex. The sewer underneath was open and sometimes the wind blew from the wrong direction.

There were no bedsheets. The Africans brought their own blankets. There were no "wards" as the term is used elsewhere. There were long, bungalowlike affairs with small cubicles. When a patient came to the Hospital, he was generally accompanied by his entire family. The mother did the cooking, as she would at home. The children were usually on their own.

The difficulty, of course, was with the term "hospital" as applied to the Schweitzer colony. It created false images and expectations. The proper term should be "jungle clinic." Dr. Schweitzer did not come to Africa for the purpose of building a towering medical center. He came in order to meet the Africans on their own terms. What he built was an African village attached to a functional medical and surgical clinic. The Africans were attracted to Schweitzer because of the man himself and because this was a village and a way of life familiar to them rather than a forbidding building where they would be cut off from their families and frightened by a world of total whiteness, of people and walls and machines. Modern medicine has come to accept the emotional security of the patient as a vital part of any therapy. Dr. Schweitzer knew this almost a half-century earlier when he made his plans to serve in Africa.

Our short walking tour finally brought us to the long single-story bungalow, consisting of about twelve rooms for staff members, where I was to stay.

The Doctor opened the door to my room, and bade me rest a while. He apologized in French for the fact that he didn't speak English and said that the only place in the world where he would dare to speak English was Edinburgh, for the people there had a habit of speaking very slowly.

I thanked the Doctor and began to tell him how privileged I felt at being able to be with him at his Hospital. He cut me short with a wave of his hand, saying with a smile, *"Pas de compliments* (no compliments) ."

The room was far nicer than I had expected. Walls and furniture were painted white. The room was only six or seven feet wide but it had everything one might need: small writing table and oil lamp, bookshelf, wooden cabinet for clothes, a stand for water basin, pitcher, and toilet articles. The bed was an iron four-poster, fairly narrow, with thin mattress. It was firm, just the way I like it, and did not sag.

One end of the room was screened in and opened out on the slope going down to the clinic and the Hospital wards. Beyond was the river Ogowe, shimmering in the midday sun. Some Africans in their pirogues were drifting downstream. It was warm, but not uncomfortably so. I was delighted with my first fifteen minutes in Lambaréné.

Later that evening I dined by candlelight at a long table with Schweitzer and the Hospital's small staff of doctors and nurses. It was a heady, high-hearted occasion: the champagne flowed freely, as did the conversation, which veered off into playwriting and acting, and from there into exploration and geology, and finally into furniture-making. On each subject the Doctor would listen carefully and then come forward with a surprising wealth of observation backed with historical information, dates, and intricate detail. With respect to furniture, the Doctor identified the softwoods and the hardwoods, spoke vividly of their uses, the relative expense involved in their manufacture, and the competitive problems in the world market for fine woods.

Whenever the conversation seemed on the verge of getting too heavy, the Doctor restored the mood of gaiety with an amusing anecdote, which invariably had a point to make. One of these anecdotes grew out of a question on the declining powers of observation of older people.

"Naturally, it all depends on the person you are talking about," he said with mock seriousness. "When I was a boy of sixteen, I was very much under my grandfather's thumb. One day a cousin of my age of whom I was very fond came to visit me. We wanted to leave the house for a certain purpose but feared Grandfather might not give us permission. And so we told him we wanted to visit our uncle some blocks distant, and he said we might go.

"When we were out of viewing range from the house, we turned sharply and went in the direction of our real destination—a beer tavern. After we had been there about ten minutes a man sat down at our table. It was our grandfather.

" 'An old man isn't as blind as you might think,' my grandfather said. 'And sometimes he is just as thirsty as younger men. Why didn't you invite me to come with you in the first place? Now pour me a drink.' "

Then Dr. Schweitzer looked at me with a twinkle in his eye.

"I'd better be careful," he said, "or Mr. Cousins will think I do nothing except tell funny stories."

The meal came to an end. The Doctor reached up and took his napkin out from his open collar, folded it carefully, and put it in his holder. The hymnbooks were passed out and the Doctor announced the number of the hymn to be sung that night.

It was then that I experienced the shock of watching him sit down to play the dilapidated old upright piano. But all the others were long accustomed to both the sight and sound, and it did not diminish the general festive air of the party. And so tonight they sang with added spirit, still flushed with the brightness of the occasion. The Doctor finished the hymn, returned to his place and read the Lord's Prayer in German. Then, the dinner over, the staff went to the small side tables, each carrying an extra cup of coffee or tea, so the mood would not be broken, and they could chat and relax in the cool of the evening.

The Doctor said good night and went back to his room to submit himself to the inevitable tyranny of his correspondence.

I walked back to my room, turned on the oil lamp, and wrote home to my wife Ellen· and my little girls. I was anxious for them to know about a place called Lambaréné and the people who worked there. For nothing is more essential to young people than to have their natural idealism nourished—and this I felt I could give them through what I had seen in my first day at Lambaréné.

Long after I turned off the small light from the kerosene lamp, I lay in bed listening to the sounds from the open wards a short distance away. There was a hacking cough, then a child's cry. They were contrasting sounds to the ones I had heard a short time earlier in the dining room, but it was part of the human mixture and it was real.

Toward the end of my visit to Lambaréné, I gave Dr. Schweitzer a message from a fifteen-year-old American boy,

Marc Chalufour, who lived in Concord, New Hampshire. Young Chalufour was engaged in a crusade to keep an old organ in his church from being replaced with an electronic instrument. He felt the old organ could be repaired, and that it was sacrilegious to let it die—especially since he did not feel the new machine was really an organ. When, through one of his teachers who was a friend of mine, he happened to learn of my coming visit to Lambaréné, he asked if I would deliver a letter from him to the Doctor. His letter identified the old organ according to make and year, and described its condition. Marc felt that if he could have a note of support from Dr. Schweitzer, he might win over the elders.

Twenty-five years ago, as a youth myself deeply interested in the organ, I had dreamed that it might some day be possible to talk to Albert Schweitzer about the art of organ building. No man alive knew more about the Silbermann organ—the finest church organ up through the nineteenth century. And now, a letter from a fifteen-year-old boy was the open sesame. To my great delight, Schweitzer spoke at length about the wonders of the Silbermann organ, about the knowledge and craftsmanship that went into it, about its tone and its unique features, about methods for keeping it in good working conditon.

Then, with obvious relish, he reached for paper and pen, and wrote a letter to Marc Chalufour:

Dear Marc:

If the organ was made in 1858, it is a good one. That was an age of fine organ building in Germany, France, England, and the United States. The period of good organ construction lasted from 1850 to 1885. After that, organs were built in factories. The organs built in the 1850's had an excellent tone—sweet, not too strong, but noble. If your church organ is still in reasonably good physical condition, it is certainly worth conserving and restoring, for it is most valuable.

In Alsace, there are organs dating from 1730 that are still in use in the churches; and if your church does not want the organ, perhaps you may be able to find a place for it yourself. One day its value will be realized. The old organs are better because they were built by artisans. In those days there was not the competition in price that there is today. The organ builder was able to use the finest material and did not have to count the hours necessary to put into it, as one has to do today. He could deliver an instrument of the highest quality.

Good luck from my heart to the courageous and intelligent young man who wants to save an organ.

Albert Schweitzer

The Doctor put down his pen; the conversation about the organ and the letter had taken the better part of an hour. Despite the expenditure of precious time, I had no regrets for having opened up the subject; he had enjoyed himself thoroughly.

We went off to dinner, at the end of which several members of the staff remarked that they had seldom seen the Doctor in such a joyous mood.

What will the historical verdict be on Albert Schweitzer? In establishing a medical center in the heart of Africa, Albert Schweitzer subordinated careers as organist and organ builder, musicologist, theologian, philosopher, and historian. His initial funds came from his book on Johann Sebastian Bach. Much of the carpentering he did himself. What he build was not a "hospital" in the Western sense;

he built an African village in which medical care was available to people most in need of it. He knew that Africans would be apprehensive about coming to a frosty white modern clinic. He wanted to meet the Africans on their own terms. He had a concept of human purpose that didn't permit a life of comfortable theorizing—even about matters of the gravest importance for renowned philosophers or theologians. He also had ideas about the nature of Christianity that didn't completely coincide with what he had been taught as a student. These ideas were related to a concept of the indwelling God and the way the reality of human brotherhood asserted itself. Rather than teach other students what he himself could not accept, he decided to leave the seminary and make his life his argument. If what he believed had genuine validity, it would be proved in his work.

There was something else. Albert Schweitzer had insight into the way pain diminished human beings. With it came a direct, unsentimental acceptance of personal responsibility to try to reduce the weight of that pain.

For a half-century, Albert Schweitzer gave the totality of himself to this design. No one knows how many thousands of sick people came to his hospital over the years. Expectant mothers fleeing from witch doctors who wanted to beat the evil out of their swollen bellies; lepers by the scores in need of a haven; men unable to stand upright because of strangulated hernias; malaria victims of all ages—all these were part of the human procession of pain that came to Albert Schweitzer in Lambaréné.

Still, there are those who will tell you that there was something dubious or unmeritorious about Schweitzer's hospital project. They will contend that the hospital was the creature of extraordinary publicity, and that the Doc-

tor was arbitrary and autocratic, especially toward the
Africans. Or they will bypass the hospital altogether and say
it is a shame he squandered his talent in the jungle. They
will say that his theology, however impressive it may have
been a half-century ago, lacks sophistication today. Or that
his philosophy has borrowed too heavily from Hegel. Or
that his reputation as Bach authority or organist or organ
builder draws on the public's capacity for being impressed
by extraordinary versatility.

But none of these questions is relevant or vital. For they
all miss the main point about Schweitzer. The main point
has nothing to do with the sanitation at Lambaréné or
Schweitzer's alleged autocratic attitudes, whether toward
blacks or whites. Nor has the real point anything to do
with the level of sophistication of his theology or philosophy, or his rank as musician or organ technician. There are
solid grounds for according him high honor and distinction in all these professions and undertakings; but again,
this is not really the central and overriding fact about
Schweitzer.

The main point about Schweitzer is that he helped
make it possible for twentieth-century man to unblock
his moral vision. There is a tendency in a relativistic age
for man to pursue all sides of a question as an end in itself,
finding relief and even refuge in the difficulty of defining
good and evil. The result is a clogging of the moral sense, a
certain feeling of self-consciousness or even discomfort
when questions with ethical content are raised. Schweitzer
furnished the nourishing evidence that nothing is more
natural in life than a moral response, which exists inde-
pendently of precise definition, its use leading not to ex-
haustion but to new energy.

The greatness of Schweitzer—indeed the essence of

Schweitzer—was the man as symbol. More important than what he did for others was what others have done because of him and the power of his example. At least a half-dozen hospitals in impoverished, remote areas have been established because of him. Wherever the Schweitzer story was known, lives were changed. A manufacturer in the American Midwest read about Schweitzer, sold his farm-implement manufacturing company, and used the money to build a string of medical clinics in the Cameroons. A Japanese professor raised money in Schweitzer's name and started an orphanage. A young German medical-school graduate, with no means or resources save a fund of inspiration, went to South America and started a hospital. Tom Dooley and his hospital in Laos are now well on the way to becoming an American legend. A beautiful, talented young Dutch girl learned about Schweitzer and selected a medical career. Six years later she was chief surgeon at the Schweitzer Hospital in Lambaréné. She left several years ago to found a hospital of her own, in Southern France, carrying on in the Schweitzer tradition.

And there is also the story of Larimer and Gwen Mellon and the work they are doing in Schweitzer's name in Haiti.

At the age of thirty-seven, Larimer Mellon was making a career out of being a rich man's son. Just bearing the Mellon name was something of a full-time job. When he read about Schweitzer, the effect was explosive; it blasted him out of one life and into a totally different one. He returned to college to complete his undergraduate education, sitting in classes alongside students half his age. Then he enrolled in medical school.

At forty-four, he received his medical diploma. With his wife, Gwen, he decided to found a hospital dedicated to Schweitzer. They selected Haiti not solely because of the high disease rate and the illiteracy of the people but because it was part of North America, very close to the most prosperous nation in the world. Some seventy miles north of Port-au-Prince, in Haiti, Larimer and Gwen Mellon selected the site of what was to become the Albert Schweitzer Hospital of Haiti.

Then there is the case of a young American named Fergus Pope. Less than a decade ago, he was traveling through Africa on a motorcycle safari. Out of curiosity, he stopped at the Schweitzer Hospital. That visit changed the entire course of his life. He returned to school, completed his undergraduate requirements, something he had not previously intended to do, worked his way through medical school in London, served his internship in a New Jersey hospital, and returned to Lambaréné as a fully accredited physician to make good his promise to himself. In the meantime he had married and become the father of three children. He brought his entire family with him to the Schweitzer Hospital. Dr. Schweitzer was overjoyed at the presence of the children at the hospital. The entire staff, in fact, was caught up in the adventure of having a young American family on the hospital grounds.

What was it about Schweitzer that caused Larimer and Gwen Mellon, Ruth and Fergus Pope, and all the others, to set their lives on a new course? It was the enduring proof Schweitzer furnished that we need not torment ourselves about the nature of human purpose. The scholar, he once wrote, must not live for science alone, nor the businessman for his business, nor the artist for his art. If affirmation for life is genuine, it will "demand from all that they should sacrifice a portion of their own lives for others."

Thus, Schweitzer's main achievement was a simple one.

He was willing to make the ultimate sacrifice for a moral principle. As with Gandhi, the power of his appeal was in renunciation. And because he was able to feel a supreme identification with other human beings he exerted a greater force than armed men on the march. It is unimportant whether we call Schweitzer a great religious figure or a great moral figure or a great philosopher. It suffices that his words and works are known and that he is loved and has influence because he enabled men to discover mercy in themselves. Early in his life he was accused of being an escapist. He was criticized for seeming to patronize the people he had chosen to serve. Yet the proof of his genuineness and his integrity is to be found in the response he awakened in people. He reached countless millions who never saw him but who were able to identify themselves with him because of the invisible and splendid fact of his own identification with them.

We live at a time when people seem afraid to be themselves, when they seem to prefer a hard, shiny exterior to the genuineness of deeply felt emotion. Sophistication is prized and sentiment is dreaded. It is made to appear that one of the worst blights on a reputation is to be called a do-gooder. The literature of the day is remarkably devoid of themes on the natural goodness or even the potential goodness of man, seeing no dramatic power in the most powerful fact of the human mixture. The values of the time lean to a phony toughness, casual violence, cheap emotion; yet we are shocked when youngsters confess to having tortured and killed because they enjoyed it and because they thought it was the thing to do.

It mattered not to Schweitzer or to history that he would be dismissed by some as a do-gooder or as a sentimental fool who frittered his life away on Africans who couldn't read or write. Schweitzer brought the kind of spirit to Africa that the black man hardly knew existed in the white man. Before Schweitzer, white skin meant beatings and gunpoint rule and the imposition of slavery on human flesh. If Schweitzer had done nothing else in his life than to accept the pain of these people as his own, he would have achieved eminence. And his place in history will rest on something more substantial than an argument over an un-swept floor in a hospital ward in the heart of Africa. It will rest on the spotless nature of his vision and the clean sweep of his nobility.

The tragedy of life is not in the hurt to a man's name or even in the fact of death itself. The tragedy of life is in what dies inside a man while he lives—the death of gen-uine feeling, the death of inspired response, the death of the awareness that makes it possible to feel the pain or the glory of other men in oneself. Schweitzer's aim was not to dazzle an age but to awaken it, to make it comprehend that moral splendor is part of the gift of life, and that each man has unlimited strength to feel human oneness and to act upon it. He proved that although a man may have no jurisdiction over the fact of his existence, he can hold supreme command over the meaning of existence for him. Thus, no man need fear death; he need fear only that he may die without having known his greatest power—the power of his free will to give his life for others.

The individual in today's world feels cut off from the large forces or movements that determine his future. This leads to fatalism and default. Schweitzer demonstrated that one man can make a difference. He had no specific pre-scription or formula for the individual. All he hoped for was that the individual would be able to peel off the layers of hardened artificialities that separate him from his real self. Man's resources do not exist outside him. His responses must come from within. A thinking and feeling man is not a helpless man. The sense of paralysis proceeds not so much out of the mammoth size of the problem but out of the puniness of purpose.

It may be said that only a Schweitzer had the knowledge and personal power to answer satisfactorily the question: "What can one man do?" Certainly we can't all be Schweitzers. But what should concern us is not what it takes to be a Schweitzer but what it takes to be a man. Nature has not been equally lavish with her endowments, but each man has his own potential in terms of achievement and service. The awareness of that potential is the discovery of purpose; the fulfillment of that potential is the discovery of strength.

For Albert Schweitzer, the assertion of this potential was not directed to charity but to justice. Also, moral reparations. "We are burdened with a great debt. We are not free to confer benefits on these people, or not confer them, as we please. It is our duty. Anything we give them is not benevolence but atonement. That is the foundation from which all deliberations about 'works of mercy' must begin."

As for the right time to act? The time, inevitably, is now. It can only be now. "Truth has no special time of its own," he said. When circumstances seem least propitious, that is the correct time.

Much of the ache and the brooding unhappiness in modern man is the result of his difficulty in using himself fully. He performs compartmentalized tasks in a compartmentalized world. He is reined in—physically, socially, spiritually. Only rarely does he have a sense of fulfilling himself through total contact with a total challenge. He finds it difficult to make real connection even with those who are near him. But there are vast urges of conscience, natural purpose, and goodness inside him demanding air and release. And he has his own potential, the regions of which are far broader than he can even guess at—a potential that keeps nagging at him to be fully used.

Albert Schweitzer was fully grown, fully developed, fully used. Did this make him happy? The question is irrelevant. He was less concerned with happiness than with purpose. What is it that has to be done? What is the best way of doing it? How does a man go about developing an inner awareness of important needs outside himself? How does he attach himself to those needs? Is he able to recognize the moral summons within him? To the extent that the individual is unconcerned about these questions, or lives apart from them, he is unfulfilled and only partly alive.

One night at the hospital, long after most of the oil lamps had been turned out, I walked down toward the river. It was a sticky night and I couldn't sleep. As I passed the compound near Dr. Schweitzer's quarters, I could hear the rapid piano movements of a Bach toccata. The Doctor was playing on the upright piano next to his bedside.

I approached the Doctor's bungalow and stood for perhaps five minutes outside the latticed window, through which I could see his silhouette in the dimly lit room. The piano had an organ footboard attachment so that he could keep his feet in playing condition. While he played the toccata his feet moved over the footboard with speed and certainty. His powerful hands were in total control of the piano as he met Bach's demands for complete definition of each note—each with its own weight and value, yet all of them laced intimately together to create an ordered whole.

I had a stronger sense of listening to a great console than if I had been in the world's largest cathedral. The yearning for an ordered beauty; the search for a creative abandonment, yet an abandonment inside a disciplined artistry; the desire to recreate a meaningful past; the need for outpouring and release, catharsis—all these things inside Albert Schweitzer spoke in his playing. And when he was through, he sat with his hands resting lightly on the keys, his great head bent forward as though to catch any echoes.

He was now freed of the pressures and tensions of the hospital, with its forms to fill out in triplicate; freed of the mounds of unanswered mail; freed of the heat and the saturating moisture of the Equator. Johann Sebastian Bach had made it possible for Albert Schweitzer to come to Lambaréné in the first place; it was Schweitzer's books on Bach that provided royalties to support the hospital in the early years. Now Bach was restoring him to a world of creative and ordered splendor.

The Doctor knew in some way that I was standing outside, listening to him play, for when he finished the toccata he called out to me by name and asked me to come in. For one half-hour or so, we chatted in the thin light of the oil lamp near the piano. He was speaking personally now—about his hopes mostly. First, he would like to see his hospital in complete running order. Second, he would like to be able to train others to run the hospital after he was gone. Third, he would like to have just a little time to work quietly and finish his two books. One was his major theological work, *The Kingdom of God*. The other was his final volume on *The Philosophy of Civilization*.

He did not wish these longings of his to give the impression he was unhappy in his work. Now and then something would happen that would give him a sense of fulfillment and deep reward. Only a few days earlier, for example, he had received a letter from a professorial colleague in France about an examination paper turned in by a nineteen-year-old boy. One of the questions on the examination was worded: "How would you define the best hope for the culture of Europe?" The boy had written: "It is not in any part of Europe. It is in a small African village and it belongs to a man in his eighties."

Dr. Schweitzer looked up from the letter. "At times like this, when the hospital has gone to sleep and everything is at peace, it makes me proud that a young man would think as he does, whether what he thinks is true or not. But in the morning, when the sun is up and the cries from the hospital are sounded, I do not think of such fancy ideas. I have all I can do to sit still while reality stares me in the face. And sometimes, if I am lucky, I can stare back."

If there is a need in America today, it is for Schweitzers among us. We are swollen with meaningless satisfactions and dulled by petty immediacies—but the threat to this nation and its freedoms and to human life in general has never been greater. To the extent that part of this threat is recognized, it is assumed it can be adequately met by a posture of military and material strength. But the crisis is basically moral and demands moral strength.

We can't save the nation by acting as though only the nation is in jeopardy, nor by acting as though the highest value is the nation. The highest value is the human being and the human potential. In order to safeguard this human potential we have to do more than to surround ourselves with high explosives. We have to make the supreme identification with other people, including those who are different from us or who have less than we. If sacrifice is required, we shall have to sacrifice. If we are to lead, what we say and what we do must become more important in our own minds than what we sell or what we use. At a time when men possess the means for demolishing a planet the only business that makes sense is the business of inspired purpose.

We live in eternal dread of hunger; but we shall never escape the hunger inside us if we are starved for inspiration or are empty of vital purpose. And if we see not at all into these things, the things that make for a single body of all those who now live or who have ever lived, then we shall have lived only half a life. It is in this sense that Albert Schweitzer has helped to make men whole.

We can rejoice in this, for Schweitzer has given an infusion of spiritual energy to our age that is real and that will persist.

Returning home, I felt happy that my two specific purposes in going to Lambaréné had been met. But even more important was the fact that the image of Albert Schweitzer I carried away with me was intact—fortified, if anything, by a direct view. For at Lambaréné I learned that a man does not have to be an angel to be a saint.

10

Harry S Truman

By FRANK GERVASI

HARRY S (no middle name, just initial) TRUMAN; born Lamar, Missouri, May 8, 1884; son of John Anderson Truman and Martha Ellen Young Truman; educated public schools, Independence, Mo.; successively worked for railroad and in banks, became farmer, active in politics as Democrat, commissioned in National Guard and commanded field artillery battery in France during World War I, continued in Army Reserve after war and rose to colonel, established unsuccessful men's clothing store in Kansas City, elected county court judge and presiding judge county court, elected United States Senate, served as chairman of Special Committee to Investigate the National Defense Program, elected Vice President of the United States, succeeded Franklin D. Roosevelt as 33rd President of the United States on Roosevelt's death, made decision to use atomic bombs against Japan, enunciated Truman Doctrine and established Marshall Plan, elected President 1948, decided to send American forces to Korea when North Korea invaded, retired 1952, succeeded by Dwight D. Eisenhower.

Frank Gervasi covered the Truman administration as Washington correspondent for Collier's *magazine. His career as a foreign correspondent began in 1934 as Universal Service correspondent in Spain. During World War II, he joined* Collier's *and covered every major action in the Medi-terranean theatre. In 1949, he helped administer the Mar-shall Plan in Italy as information chief. Subsequently, he wrote a syndicated column for the New York* Post *and* Worldwide Press Service. *He is the author of a number of books.*

M EASURED BY THE MAGNITUDE of the events of the seven crucial years of his incumbency, Harry S Truman was un-doubtedly one of our "greatest" Presidents. Indeed, few if any of his predecessors made so many far-reaching, his-torically important decisions. His era, which began at pre-cisely 7:09 P.M. on the evening of April 12, 1945, a few hours after the death of Franklin D. Roosevelt, witnessed changes in American foreign policy that ranked in im-portance with the promulgation of the Monroe Doctrine and the decisions to enter two World Wars.

In Truman's time, the first atom bomb was dropped, victory was achieved over the Axis powers, the Marshall Plan was launched, America's policy of containment of communist expansion in Europe and Asia was formulated and applied, the North Atlantic Treaty Organization was created, the United States intervened militarily in the Greek Civil War and in support of Korean independence and last, but by no means least, General Douglas A. Mac-Arthur, considered by many "the greatest living Ameri-can," was fired for flouting presidential authority.

Some students of the presidency already rate Truman with Washington, Jefferson, Lincoln, Wilson and the two Roosevelts in presidential stature. Future historians may not agree, but whatever their final judgment none will deny his courage or political skill. Only a courageous man could have made the hard decisions that characterized his era; only a skillful politician could have bulled through Congress the costly programs which he sponsored, or could have so clamorously defeated Thomas E. Dewey in 1948 in a national election whose outcome confounded the public opinion polls and baffled the victor's critics.

Truman came to power at a critical juncture in the country's history, with victory yet to be won in mankind's bloodiest and costliest war and a peace yet to be made. Whoever led the nation held in his hands the destinies of some 150,000,000 Americans and would influence for good or evil the lives of about 2,500,000,000 other inhabitants of the rest of the world.

Of all this Truman was humbly aware that fateful April evening in 1945 as he stood in the austere Cabinet Room of the White House, pressed a damp palm on a Bible and swore before Chief Justice of the Supreme Court Harlan Stone to uphold the Constitution. But he sincerely wished, at that moment, that the burden had fallen on someone else. The next day he told reporters that he had felt as though "the moon, the stars and all the planets" had fallen on him.

Politically, Truman had never aspired beyond a seat in the Senate and, as vice president, he had never allowed his mind to dwell on the fact that he was only a heartbeat away from the presidency. Militarily, all he knew of war was what he had learned as an artillery officer in 1917–1918, for, during his scant fourteen weeks as vice president, he had not yet been invited to the meetings of the Joint Chiefs of Staff and did not know that his country possessed the atom bomb. Although FDR had filled him in on the details of the Yalta Agreement, the President had not seen fit to confide the secret of the bomb. Moreover,

Truman was untraveled and his knowledge of America's relations with foreign nations was limited.

"Nobody," he said later, "ever briefed me for the job. I had to learn it from the ground up."

In the context of American history, Truman reminded most observers of Andrew Johnson. Like the tailor who succeeded Lincoln in another April back in 1865, the man who came after Roosevelt inherited uniquely huge, complex problems. But where Johnson was charged with the rebuilding of a nation, Truman faced the task of reconstructing an entire world. Where Johnson had dealt in mere millions, Truman would deal in multi-billions. And, like Johnson, the new President realized that whatever he did would be judged by what his prestigious predecessor might have done.

Truman was the loneliest man in America when the members of FDR's cabinet crowded around him after the swearing-in ceremonies. But the people in the streets waved to him encouragingly the morning he rode to the White House to go to work as President for the first time. They sympathized with him for having been so suddenly confronted with the towering problems of an unfinished war and an unsecured peace. His presence in the White House tempered the grief of his predecessor's mourners and assuaged the venom of those who hated FDR.

Democrats and Republicans, liberals and conservatives, workers and industrialists cheered the new chief. The political left was warmed by Truman's across-the-board New Deal voting record in the Senate and the right was encouraged by his known conservatism in economic matters. Labor confidently expected higher wages and management anticipated higher profits.

For a while, Truman appeared to please everyone in

what looked like a politically fortuitious love match between him and the people. The honeymoon endured through the eventful spring and summer of 1945, as triumphant headlines recorded the founding of the United Nations at San Francisco, the victory over the Nazis, the dropping of the atomic bomb on Hiroshima and Nagasaki, the fall of the Japanese Empire and the promises of permanent peace, which later proved illusory, raised by the Potsdam conference.

Americans readily identified with the uncommonly modest Harry S Truman, seeing in him a projection of the sum of themselves, approximating Mr. Average Man far more closely than his sophisticated, aristocratic predecessor. Truman clearly was neither sophisticated nor aristocratic. Actually, he came closer than anyone since Lincoln to fulfilling the cherished "log cabin to White House" tradition of the presidency.

Born at Lamar, Missouri, on May 8, 1884, the grandson of Kentucky pioneers, Harry S Truman grew up on his father John's farm in Grandview and attended high school in Independence. He never went to college. Rejected as a candidate for West Point because of poor eyesight, he joined the Missouri National Guard in 1905 and ran his family's six hundred acre Jackson County farm until 1917, when he entered the Fort Sill Field Artillery School in Oklahoma. There he was commissioned as a first lieutenant but by the time the United States entered World War I, Truman had achieved the rank of captain. He went overseas with Battery D, 129th Field Artillery, served with distinction in the Vosges, Meuse-Argonne and St. Mihiel actions and was discharged in 1919 as a major.

On his return from France, Truman wooed and won his childhood sweetheart, Elizabeth Virginia Wallace, the only daughter of David Willock Wallace. Harry and Bess, as he called her, had been graduated together from the same grammar and high schools in Independence. They were married June 28, 1919.

At about that time, Truman went into the haberdashery business in Kansas City, but in the postwar recession the enterprise faltered and failed. Characteristically, Truman refused to go into bankruptcy and insisted on paying his creditors off in full at considerable hardship to himself. His friends advised him to enter politics and introduced him to Tom Pendergast. This political boss of Missouri's powerful Kansas City–based Democratic machine took a liking to the dapper, open-faced ex-farmer with the astigmatic blue-grey eyes and saw to it that in 1922 Truman was elected county judge of eastern Jackson County. Because he was not a lawyer, Truman promptly enrolled in the Kansas City School of Law and qualified in 1925.

In 1924, the year Mrs. Truman gave birth to their daughter Margaret, Truman was defeated for re-election, partly because he opposed the local Ku Klux Klan, but he returned to the court as presiding judge in 1927. His duties involved supervision of expenditures of all highway moneys. During the next seven years, he rebuilt Jackson County's roads and earned a reputation as an able jurist and an incorruptible administrator. The farm-bred Missourian did not know it, but he was on the highroad to Washington and the presidency.

In 1934, the self-educated lawyer was nominated for the United States Senate and won easily, with the help of the Pendergast machine. In time, he would be known as "The Man from Independence," but, on his arrival in the Capital as the junior Senator from Missouri, he was known as "The Man from Pendergast." In fact, Truman's political career seemed at an end when his sponsor went to prison in 1939 for income tax evasion. But, in 1940, Truman amazed everyone by getting himself re-elected—not with the help of the discredited Pendergast machine, but by attracting the votes of farmers, workers and Negroes with his honestly liberal stance on local issues.

Truman, however, still seemed destined for political oblivion until, in 1941, he became chairman of a special Senate committee investigating waste in defense spending. By the time the investigation ended in 1944, the Missourian had saved the United States government an estimated $1,000,000,000. His good work won him little national attention, but did not go unnoticed at the White House. Roosevelt picked Truman as his running mate for his fourth try at the presidency. The Missourian was still so obscure a figure that, when the President told Admiral William Leahy of his choice for second place on the Democratic ticket, the then Chief of Staff exclaimed, "Who the hell is Harry Truman?" A few months later, America and the world knew him as the thirty-second President of the United States.

When the war ended, so did Truman's honeymoon with the press, the legislators on Capitol Hill, industry, labor and some, though not all, of the electorate. Crisis piled on crisis in an unhappy pyramid of presidential grief. Industry demanded higher prices and labor clamored for higher wages. Veterans hungered for jobs and houses. Mothers, wives and sweethearts wanted their men home from the war right away. The nearly bankrupt British asked for a huge loan. The Zionists pleaded for a Jewish national homeland in Palestine. Civil wars erupted in China and Indonesia. Relations among the "Big Three" (the U.S., Britain and Soviet Russia) deteriorated. All Europe cried for food.

"Every week," the President said, "you think that maybe the next won't be quite so hectic. But the coming week is just a little more so. There's always a crisis around the corner that I have to do something about."

Suddenly, the man who could do no wrong, whose popularity at times exceeded even Roosevelt's, could do no right. His increasing maturity, his patience and kindliness, his integrity—even his actual skill in handling problems so complex that they would have taxed the abilities of far more experienced men—did not emerge in the newspapers' accounts of the activities of the presidency after V-J Day. Instead, the character of the new President, as drawn by a suddenly critical press, was that of a leader who chafed under the responsibilities of a job he had not wanted, had a "program but no policy," could not make a good speech, appointed inept cronies to important government posts, had lost control of Congress and was overfond of poker and bourbon whisky.

When he made mistakes, the President's more vicious critics punned that "to err is only Truman," and he was unflatteringly compared to Warren G. Harding. Nevertheless, the new President could point to a record of positive achievement.

In the domestic field, Truman shook up the economic high command and started a campaign to fight the nation's worst internal enemy, inflation. Only unlimited production, the President knew, could forestall disaster. War-accumulated dollars burned in people's pockets and the demand for consumer goods was enormous. To stimulate production, Truman removed restrictions on raw materials for washing machines, automobiles, radios and countless other consumer items. As a further incentive to industry, he reduced corporate taxes and abolished the excess profits tax.

But it was in the international field that Harry S Truman made his mark in history. America took its place in the United Nations and agreed to participate in the Bretton Woods plan for restoring the production and purchasing powers of war-ravaged nations. To that end, the government expanded the lending facilities of the Export-Import Bank from $700,000,000 to $3,500,000,000, and the reciprocal-trade agreements with Latin America were extended. The life of the wartime United Nations Relief and Rehabilitation Administration was lengthened; UNRRA was given funds with which to help war sufferers back onto their feet and so begin the reconstruction of a war-scarred world.

Then, after struggling for nearly two years to find an accommodation with Russia, Truman undertook a bold program aimed at no less than arresting further post-Potsdam Soviet expansion in Europe and the Near East. The idea of containing communist expansion was devised to meet the threat of Soviet domination of the eastern Mediterranean.

It is not clear, even from Truman's memoirs, exactly when he decided that collaboration with Russia had become impossible. But it was common knowledge at the time that Truman never fully shared his predecessor's hopes of successful cooperation and that, as early as January of 1946, only nine months after he became President, he was being warned by his advisers of Soviet ambitions in the Middle East, specifically in Greece and Turkey. Chief of Staff Admiral Leahy and Navy Secretary James Forrestal were pressing him to re-establish American naval power in the eastern Mediterranean to thwart Russian designs. Truman was also greatly influenced by former Prime Minister Winston Churchill, who warned the free world of aggressive Soviet intentions in his famous "Iron Curtain" speech at Fulton, Missouri, on March 5, 1946, and by Ambassador Averell Harriman, who reported on Soviet plans and ambitions from Moscow.

But it was George Kennan, then Counselor of Embassy in Moscow, who elaborated the assumptions behind the containment policy.

On February 9, 1946, Stalin had declared that international peace was impossible "under the present capitalist development of world economy" and ominously called upon the Russian people to prepare for "any eventuality." Kennan sent a long dispatch to Washington detailing his view of the character, tactics, motivation and probable objectives of the Soviet Union and of international communism. Kennan concluded that Russia represented "a political force committed fanatically to the belief that with the U.S. there can be no permanent modus vivendi."

If, as Kennan and others said, the Soviet leaders and their followers were working to promote the violent overthrow of non-communist governments, it behooved the United States to devise some means of meeting the threat. Kennan elaborated the doctrine of containment in an anonymous article in the July 1947 issue of *Foreign Affairs* in which he stated that the United States could live at peace with the Soviet Union only by building its own strength and by erecting effective counterweights in order to contain communist power at least in Europe. "To avoid destruction," Kennan wrote, "the United States need only measure up to its own best traditions and prove itself worthy of preservation as a great nation."

Truman and his new Secretary of State, George C. Marshall, heeded the warnings sounded by Kennan and the others who favored the containment policy. By the late winter of 1946–47, the Soviet threat in the eastern Mediterranean and the Middle East had become very real. Moscow was exerting extraordinary diplomatic pressure on Turkey for cession of certain territory and the right to build naval bases in the Bosphorus, threatening dire consequences if Turkey refused to yield. The Kremlin, although now occupied by communists, seemed as determined to achieve control of the Dardanelles and the eastern Mediterranean as its Czarist occupants from the days of Peter the Great onward.

Meanwhile, civil war had broken out in Greece between rightists and leftists. Since early 1944, the British had supported the right-wing Greek government in its protracted, bloody effort to suppress an anti-monarchist revolt of republicans and other leftist elements led by a communist faction known as EAM. Britain informed Washington, on February 24, 1947, that she could no longer bear the burden of resisting communist expansion in the eastern Mediterranean and would have to withdraw from Greece.

This marked the end of historic British supremacy in one of the most strategic areas in the world. Truman's prompt response marked an equally fateful turning point in American foreign policy, for it would lead, inevitably, to similar decisions in Asia. "If Greece was lost," the President said later, "Turkey would become an untenable outpost in a sea of communism. Similarly, if Turkey yielded to Soviet demands, the position of Greece would be extremely endangered."

After consulting with Congressional leaders, Truman went to Capitol Hill, asked for $400,000,000 for military assistance to Greece and Turkey and enunciated what came to be known as the Truman Doctrine: "I believe that it must be the foreign policy of the United States to support free peoples who are resisting attempted subjugation by armed minorities or by outside pressures. . . . The free peoples of the world look to us for support in maintaining their freedoms. If we falter in our leadership, we may endanger the peace of the world—and we shall surely endanger the welfare of our own Nation."

It seems fairly evident that, while the real architect of containment was Kennan, the Truman Doctrine which implemented the policy went considerably beyond Kennan's precepts and laid the groundwork for subsequent American military action in Korea and, eventually, Vietnam. Indeed, the American foreign policy of the 1960s plainly had its origins in the politico-economic-military foreign policy of the Truman era.

In its eventually successful efforts to save Greece from communist domination and strengthen the Turkish bastion on the Soviet southern flank, the government spent some $659,000,000 between 1947 and 1950. But while the American task in Turkey was quickly and inexpensively accomplished, the task in Greece proved immensely more difficult and costly. The United States found itself in the embarrassing position of defending democracy by supporting a reactionary Greek government that refused to do anything effective about the basic economic and social evils that had stirred the masses in revolt. A large American military contingent and huge quantities of military supplies were required before a reorganized Greek army was able to end the civil war. Victory was not assured until Yugoslavia broke with the Soviet bloc in 1948 and abandoned support of the Greek communists in the summer of 1949.

The Greco-Turkish situation epitomized the dangers that threatened all of western Europe. France, Italy and other nations were staggering under nearly impossible economic burdens of reconstruction and facing violent political and social upheaval. Starvation and economic collapse had been prevented by some $11,000,000,000 in UNRRA aid, but while this had helped Europeans buy food, clothing and other necessities, it had not contributed to sound recovery. The situation worsened steadily until it was clear late in 1947 that, without large-scale American aid, communism might take over in France and Italy.

Clearly, the situation called for a radical remedy and the Policy Planning Staff of the State Department, headed by Kennan, worked hard to devise one. Undersecretary of State Dean Acheson provided the first clue to Washington's thinking when he said it had become imperative to strengthen all governments that were "seeking to preserve their independence, democratic institutions and human freedoms against totalitarian pressures, internal or external."

Then, in a speech at Harvard on June 5, 1947, Secretary Marshall pointed up the solution, envisaging nothing less than the reconstruction of the entire western European economy to provide the foundations for a more stable social order. He hoped that Russia might be willing to cooperate, but the Russians had been consolidating their own economic hegemony over eastern Europe since 1945 and were not likely to relinquish this control by cooperating in any western plan. Moreover, two months before Marshall's speech, the Russians demonstrated their determination to prevent solution of Europe's most immediate problem, the unification and economic rehabilitation of Germany.

Representatives from Britain, France, Italy, Turkey and the other non-communist nations met in Paris on July 12, 1947, appointed a Committee of European Economic Co-operation and two months later submitted a master recovery plan. It called for $22,400,000,000 in assistance and loans from the United States for the "struggle which was to be waged with the weapons of politics and propaganda as well as with loans, grants and trade agreements."

Truman personally led the fight to finance the European Recovery Program, as the Marshall Plan was called, against the opposition of its many opponents. He submitted the draft of the enabling legislation on December 19, 1947, calling for $17,000,000,000 in aid during the ensuing four years. Congressional opposition dissolved when a communist minority in Czechoslovakia seized control in February 1948 and destroyed a democracy which millions of free men everywhere mourned.

Republican Senator Arthur Vandenberg, a one-time isolationist, spearheaded the battle in Congress in favor of the Marshall Plan but reduced the first appropriation from $6,800,000,000 for the first fifteen months to $5,200,-000 for the first twelve months. Then, after Czechoslovakia fell to the communists, he brought his fellow Senators to their feet by declaring: "The greatest nation on earth either justifies or surrenders its leadership. We must choose . . . The iron curtain must not come to the rims of the Atlantic either by aggression or by default." The Senate approved the bill by a huge majority on March 13, the House approved the measure on March 31 and the President signed it on April 3, 1948.

The launching of the Marshall Plan, the greatest single

act of magnanimity in history, meant that thereafter the destinies of the American people were inextricably interwoven with the fate of all free peoples in a world divided and struggling for a new birth of freedom. America provided some $12,000,000,000 in assistance through 1951 and the results were astonishing. The gross national product of the Marshall Plan countries as a whole increased twenty-five percent from 1947 through 1950; industrial production rose sixty-four percent and agricultural output twenty-four percent. Indeed, in most categories recovery far exceeded the best prewar levels.

In the Marshall Plan, Harry S Truman undertook the most ambitious reconstruction program ever conceived. Its political, social and humanitarian results probably constitute his greatest single contribution to the peace and well-being of the free world.

However, western European unity and well-being depended to a degree upon the ability of European and American statesmen to devise workable plans for rehabilitating Germany and linking it to the free world. American, British, and French leaders tried hard to unify and neutralize Germany through 1947, but the Russians sternly refused to approve any agreement on Germany that did not give them virtual control of the Ruhr, industrial heart of Europe. Realizing that agreement with Russia was impossible, the western powers worked out their own plan for Germany.

Economically, German recovery was the key to European recovery; militarily, the defense of Western Germany was the key to the defense of western Europe. Britain, America and France consolidated their zones and created a West German Federal State, with its own government, though with limited authority, and with its capital in

Frankfort. West Germany was included as a full partner in the European Recovery Program and, by May 8, 1949, had elected a federal parliament (Diet) that met at Bonn in September. Germany had a full fledged, constitutional democracy for the first time since Hitler had brought about the downfall of the Republic.

Truman had been a harassed and sorrowful man when he walked on stage from the wings of vice presidential obscurity, but, by early 1948, he was the sure-handed central figure of the greatest political drama in American history—the country's emergence as a giant among nations. Although, after 1946, he was obliged to work with a Republican Congress and was confronted by partisan opposition on most issues, he was at once as serene as silk and as stubborn as a Missouri mule. Cartoonists who had characterized him as a pygmy sitting in a giant's chair, began drawing him as a victorious prize fighter. And, up on Capitol Hill, legislators who had referred to him familiarly as "Harry," now addressed him as "Mr. President." He was no longer Roosevelt's stand-in reading from a New Deal script, but his own man.

The sweeping Republican Congressional victory of 1946 was a Democratic Party "disaster," but actually the event liberated Truman. He was free to be himself. "I shall devote all my energy," Truman announced a few days after the party's November debacle, "to the discharge of my duty with a full realization of the responsibility which results from the present state of affairs." The presence on The Hill of almost as many Republicans as one might find at a nominating convention caused Truman far less concern than it did his party's strategists. "Don't worry, boys," Truman reassured them. "I'll just cooperate the living hell out of those gentlemen up there."

Meanwhile, the public opinion polls and the press registered Truman's rising popularity. If editorials in virtually every newspaper in the land except the *Daily Worker* and thousands of laudatory letters and telegrams received at the White House meant anything, he had hit the popularity jackpot with his Truman Doctrine. The country liked the way Truman had "talked back" to Joseph Stalin. Some critics feared war, but Truman did not. He sensed, correctly, that Russia was in no position to fight a war and would not be until it had satisfied the enormous demand within the Soviet Union for consumer goods, had rebuilt its industrial plants and itself owned atomic weapons at least equal to ours.

The line between diplomacy and strategy, politics and war, is always a thin one. Of this, Truman was keenly conscious, but he firmly believed that America's political destiny as the fountainhead of democracy demanded that the nation be willing to undertake whatever military risks might be involved.

"I don't care," he told friends, "what kind of governments nations achieve. They can all go communist, if they wish, provided that they do so with due respect to law and in free and unfettered elections. But we can't stand for police states imposed on free peoples by armed minorities."

Early in 1948, America and the west faced a new Soviet challenge to peace and security and, while the world held its breath, Harry S Truman once again was called upon to walk the thin line between diplomacy and strategy, politics and war. Once again, he demonstrated America's willingness to undertake enormous military risks to prevent the creation of "police states imposed on free peoples by armed minorities."

On April 1, 1948, the Soviets began restricting the

movement of people and freight from the western zones into Berlin, then under four-power control but isolated in the Russian-held eastern zone of Germany. The action was an escalation of Soviet reaction to the Marshall Plan and to western efforts to unify and rehabilitate West Germany.

Violent controversies arose in the four-power control council governing the German capital when the Soviet representatives, in retaliation against allied introduction of a new West German currency into Berlin, halted all western traffic into the city. The Soviet objectives were to force the western Allies out of their salient behind the iron curtain and to abandon their efforts to unify West Germany.

It was the first open test of strength between West and East in what soon became known as the Cold War. Retreat never entered the mind of the stubborn Missourian in the White House. After turning down an alternative suggestion that the Allies fight their way into Berlin if necessary, Truman approved a bolder plan, namely to supply West Berlin by air and oblige the Russians to decide whether there should be peace or war between West and East.

The Soviet blockade of Berlin continued from June, 1948, through the presidential election in November of that year, until mid-May of the following year. By that time, however, the U.S. and British air forces had accomplished a miracle: a daily average of 4,000 tons of supplies, including coal, had entered West Berlin and frustrated the Soviet attempt to starve the city into submission. The Russians lifted the blockade. With the West's tremendous victory in Berlin, the Soviet Union's posture in the Cold War "struggle for the soul of Europe," as Dean Acheson put it, passed from the offensive to the defensive.

Meanwhile, western European nations and the United

States joined in the creation of a counterbalance to Soviet power known as the North Atlantic Treaty Organization. The participants—the U.S., Britain, France, Italy, Holland, Belgium, Canada, Iceland, Luxembourg, Denmark, Norway and Portugal—solemnly declared that an armed attack against any member in Europe or North America would be considered an attack against all signatories. The pact was later extended to include Greece and Turkey.

In signing the treaty, the United States abandoned its historic diffidence toward "entangling alliances," and confirmed its solemn determination to protect free peoples from Soviet attack. But new, grave challenges to world peace were developing in Asia, beyond the reach of NATO. A communist victory in China upset the delicate power balance in the Far East and paved the way for the North Korean and Chinese assaults on South Korea.

Washington had been seeking a policy to meet the situation created in the Orient by the establishment of a so-called Chinese People's Republic allied to Moscow. The Truman administration might have recognized the new regime, as Britain and other powers did, but Peking had started a violent campaign in 1949 to drive American diplomats, missionaries and representatives of private business from China. The reaction throughout the United States was violent. It was intensified by "the China lobby" and by Republican efforts to have the administration extend military assistance to Chiang Kai-shek's Nationalists in Formosa.

The President had declared his determination not to be drawn into the Chinese civil war, even if Formosa fell to the Chinese communists, but, only a few days later, Secretary of State Acheson announced a new American policy in the Far East. The American government, he declared, desiring only to help the peoples of Asia to "realize their democratic aspirations," would undertake to protect a "defensive perimeter" running from the Aleutians to Japan, the Ryukyus, and the Philippines. But it could not attempt, Acheson said, to defend other areas—Korea, Formosa, and Southeast Asia—from military attack. Aggression there, Acheson concluded, would have to be met "by the peoples involved and by the United Nations."

Acheson's speech provided new ammunition for the Republican attack on the Administration. Senators Joseph McCarthy, Robert Taft, Kenneth S. Wherry and other GOP spokesmen opened a violent campaign to drive Acheson from office, charging that his State Department was riddled with communists and fellow travelers who, as Senator Taft put it, had "surrendered to every demand of Russia and promoted at every opportunity the communist cause in China." The assault wrecked bipartisanship in matters of foreign policy. It made formulation of a rational Far Eastern policy impossible precisely when it was most needed, and raised grave doubts abroad regarding the wisdom of American leadership.

Months of troubled soul-searching followed, and thoughtful men wondered whether civilization was heading for destruction when the President disclosed on September 23, 1949, that the Russians had detonated their first atom bomb. Overnight, the premises upon which American defensive strategy had been based since 1945 were rendered obsolete. A fierce debate ensued in administration circles over the development of hydrogen bombs potentially one thousand times more powerful than those that destroyed Hiroshima and Nagasaki.

On January 31, 1950, Truman announced that he had ordered the Atomic Energy Commission to proceed with work on the new bomb. Americans, though stunned by the gloomy news, agreed that their government had no other recourse. Dean Acheson declared, perhaps more prophetically than he knew, that the American people were entering upon a new era of "total diplomacy," and predicted that their fortitude and wisdom would be put to "severe and numerous tests."

Soon after Acheson enumerated America's position, South Korea was invaded by communist North Korean forces. Korea had been freed from Japanese control after World War II. No thought had been given to a postwar policy for the strategic peninsula over which Japan and Russia had historically fought for control. Clearly, Russian dominance there would gravely threaten the future security of Japan. Russian troops had entered northern Korea in the summer of 1945, while American forces had occupied southern Korea. The two powers had decided on the thirty-eighth parallel, north of Seoul, the capital, as the demarcation line between their forces. The United States had assumed that the Korean people would quickly organize a government, whereupon the occupation forces would be withdrawn. Actually, the Russians had no intention of allowing a unified Korean government to be created. They established a communist "people's government" in North Korea and trained and equipped an army of some 150,000 men.

Meanwhile, in response to an appeal by the U.S., the United Nations Assembly established a Temporary Commission on Korea and, after being denied entry into the Soviet zone, held elections in South Korea for a constituent assembly, which adopted a constitution and created a new Republic of Korea with Syngman Rhee as President. Non-communist powers (as well as the U.N.) recognized his regime as the only lawful government of Korea and the United States, on the advice of the Joint Chiefs and General MacArthur, who was then in Japan, withdrew its troops from South Korea in the summer of 1949.

North Korean forces crossed the thirty-eighth parallel in an all-out invasion of South Korea on June 25, 1950. Apparently, the American withdrawal and Acheson's statement that Korea lay outside America's far eastern "defense perimeter" had led the Kremlin to conclude that America would not fight to prevent Soviet control of the peninsula.

Truman ordered the matter brought before the U.N. Security Council, which condemned the invasion as aggression and demanded the immediate withdrawal of communist troops from South Korean territory. The President ordered the Seventh Fleet to neutralize Formosa and directed General MacArthur to furnish arms and limited air support to the South Koreans. That evening, Truman summoned his advisers and, after hearing their views, announced that American naval and air forces in the Far East would render full assistance to the South Koreans. Everything he had done in the previous years had been to avoid making just such a decision. But harder ones were yet to be made.

Truman next rallied the U.N. to a collective effort to repel the communist aggression and preserve the peace. The Security Council quickly adopted an American-sponsored resolution calling upon member nations to render all necessary assistance to the legitimate Republic of Korea. Then, on June 29 and 30, after it had become evident that the invaders would overrun the peninsula unless stopped by American troops, President Truman made still another hard decision—to send two divisions of ground troops from Japan to Korea and authorize a naval blockade of North Korea.

The Joint Chiefs, the State Department and General MacArthur all assumed that limited American support would turn the tide, and that Russia and China would not intervene. They would be proved wrong.

The President's decision to call Stalin's hand was hailed by Republican leaders, among them Governor Thomas E. Dewey of New York and John Foster Dulles, and the members of the House of Representatives rose in a body and cheered when they learned that the President had ordered air and naval forces into action in defense of South Korea.

A United Nations Command was established and nineteen nations contributed men and weapons. By the end of 1950, British, Turkish, Australian and Philippine troops were fighting beside Americans and South Koreans under the supreme command of General MacArthur. Meanwhile, however, the North Koreans almost overran the entire peninsula. The communists had pushed the defenders into the southeastern corner and were threatening to drive them out of Pusan, their only remaining supply port. But MacArthur brought in heavy American reinforcements and turned the tide. The United Nations forces reconquered all lost terrain and, by October, had regained the thirty-eighth parallel and were preparing to launch an invasion of North Korea. The American people held their breath.

The Korean War awakened Americans to the danger of new and more grave Soviet aggressions. The peril was great because America and western Europe lacked effective counterforces. Truman resisted demands for all-out mobilization, but moved swiftly toward a limited mobilization.

Congress quickly approved the basic legislation, the Defense Production Act, to "oppose acts of aggression and develop and maintain whatever military and economic strength is found necessary to carry out this purpose." The measure provided tax incentives to encourage defense production and build industrial plants and imposed limited price and credit controls. Congress appropriated $12,600,-000,000 for the defense establishment and approved plans to double the armed forces from 1,500,000 to 3,000,000 men. It also adopted a revenue bill designed to raise nearly $4,500,000,000 in additional income and corporate taxes, and appropriated over $5,000,000,000 for military aid to western Europe, chiefly to translate NATO from a blueprint to a military reality. The North Atlantic Council met in Brussels in December 1950 and approved plans for unifying all NATO forces under Truman's appointee, General Dwight Eisenhower. An American proposal for limited German rearmament was killed by French opposition.

In one of the bitterest congressional campaigns in American history that autumn, the Republicans charged that Truman had blundered badly and made the Korean War inevitable. They predicted inflation, socialization and expansion of federal power unless the Truman policies were abandoned. But the main Republican issue, raised and nourished by Senator Joseph McCarthy, was the alleged failure of the Democrats to recognize and cope with "communist infiltration and influence" in the State Department. Not all Republican leaders followed the lead of McCarthy, who used the issue to defeat Millard Tydings in Maryland just as nastily as Richard Nixon exploited it in his successful campaign for election to the Senate from California. But most Republican campaigners rode the "communist issue" with considerable success elsewhere.

The Democrats narrowly retained control of both houses in the election of November 7, 1950, but the results actually constituted a smashing defeat for the administration. Plainly, the Republicans were playing politics with the nation's destiny.

In the months that followed, the nation came dangerously close to a general war with China—what General Omar Bradley, Chairman of the Joint Chiefs, later called "the wrong war, at the wrong place, at the wrong time and with the wrong enemy." Such a war would have required the redirection of all available manpower and resources to the Far East and possibly invited a Russian assault against western Europe. Truman's Republican opponents, led by the prestigious General MacArthur, demanded it and, in fact, very nearly brought it about. Only the Missourian's courageous resistance to the demands of the opposition prevented our involvement in a conflict with China which might well have precipitated World War III.

The U.N. forces under MacArthur had driven to the thirty-eighth parallel and halted until the General Assembly called upon the general to "take all necessary steps" to establish control throughout all of Korea. The Chinese People's Republic had warned that it would not "supinely tolerate" seeing their neighbors being "savagely invaded by imperialists," and declared that "if U.S. or U.N. forces crossed the thirty-eighth parallel, China would send troops to the Korean frontier to defend North Korea."

Few free world leaders took the threat seriously. Mac-Arthur assured the President at their famous Wake Island conference that there was "little danger" of Chinese intervention and promised "a great slaughter" if the Chinese intervened. He was authorized to drive northward to the Yalu River.

But just as it seemed that North Korean resistance had collapsed, American troops encountered considerable resistance, not from North Koreans, but from Chinese "volunteers." The Peking government demanded prompt American withdrawal from Korea, but MacArthur countered with a massive United Nations offensive to drive the Chinese "volunteers" beyond the Yalu, violating his instructions to use only South Korean troops in order to avoid provoking the Chinese.

The Chinese counterattacked in force, routed Republic of Korea troops which held the center of the U.N. line, forced withdrawal of the U.S. Eighth Army on the western flank and isolated the Tenth Corps on the northeastern flank. Two weeks of desperate fighting were required before the First Marine Division, the Third and Seventh Infantry Divisions, and the ROK Capital Division were able to escape to the seaport of Hungnam, whence they were evacuated in a Korean Dunkirk.

Truman, meanwhile, began to prepare the country and the United Nations for possible general war. He denounced the Chinese intervention as "unprovoked aggression," outlined a vast mobilization program, declared a national emergency and announced creation of an Office of Defense Mobilization along with production and stabilization controls.

During the next two years, Congress opposed the President on nearly everything else, but granted his requests for unprecedented peacetime appropriations for the military establishment and military aid to NATO. The military strength of the United States increased spectacularly and the NATO countries created forces at least theoretically capable of withstanding a Soviet invasion.

This was not achieved, however, without great difficulty.

Senator Taft proposed a re-examination of the nation's foreign and military policies and questioned whether the defense of western Europe was essential to American security. Former President Herbert Hoover joined the neo-isolationist chorus with a statement that the United States should defend the Atlantic and Britain, leave the Pacific to Japan and withdraw troops from western Europe. Senator Wherry offered a resolution in Congress declaring that "no ground forces of the United States should be assigned to the European area for the purposes of the North Atlantic Treaty pending adoption of a policy with respect thereto by Congress."

Truman stood firm, asserting his well-founded belief that the western Europeans would build a strong anti-Russian barrier if the American people did not desert them. Even so, the debate raged on, especially after House Republicans publicly endorsed Hoover's proposals. In the end, Truman prevailed. The Senate reaffirmed American commitments to NATO and approved the sending of four more divisions to Europe, but warned the President not to send additional troops without "further Congressional approval."

The furor was mild, however, compared to the fury that exploded following Truman's recall of General MacArthur from his Tokyo command. The MacArthur affair, unique in American history, brought to a head the conflict over Truman's far eastern and European policies.

The conflict between the President and the general had its origins in their divergent views of relations between the U.S. and Chiang Kai-shek's government. Following a highly theatrical visit to Formosa in July 1950, MacArthur addressed a message to a convention of the Veterans of Foreign Wars calling for "incorporation of Formosa into the American security system" and advocating an "offensive strategy" in Asia. The veterans cheered, but Truman was shocked and seriously considered firing the general then and there.

Instead, Truman summoned MacArthur to Wake Island, reiterated that he had no intention of becoming involved in the Chinese civil war, and warned his general not to make any more jingoistic statements.

MacArthur kept his peace for a while, but, after the Chinese intervention in Korea, opened a campaign to pressure Truman into permitting him to bomb Chinese bases in Manchuria. He suggested that the United States blockade the Chinese coast, bombard China by air and by sea and support a Nationalist invasion from Formosa. Otherwise, he intimated, it might be necessary to evacuate his forces from Korea. Truman and the Joint Chiefs refused to permit such retaliatory actions.

Subsequent events decided the issue. The American Eighth Army, then under the command of General Matthew Ridgway, halted the enemy assault and made it evident that the U.N. forces could remain in Korea. The President and Joint Chiefs agreed upon a policy of "limited war for the limited objective" of defending South Korea to minimize the risk of a general war with China. The President and his advisers reasoned that essentially defensive operations in Korea might not destroy the Chinese communist regime, but could inflict such sufficiently terrible punishment as to induce the Chinese and North Korean forces to give up the struggle.

But MacArthur was temperamentally incapable of accepting the concept of "limited war" and was prepared to abandon Europe to its uncertain fate. He sincerely believed that America's destiny lay in the Orient. Believing, also, that blundering political leadership was depriving the American people of an opportunity to settle the Far Eastern question for generations to come, he resorted to desperate measures. When the Joint Chiefs informed him that Truman was seeking to settle the Korean conflict by diplomatic means, MacArthur replied with public statements aimed at preventing any peaceful settlement. In a letter to the Republican House minority leader, Joseph W. Martin, Jr., the general called for war against communism in the Far East, and declared: "We must win. There is no substitute for victory."

The letter was read to the House and convulsed a nation already aroused by the frenzied Republican campaign to force the administration to adopt MacArthur's proposals, though they might have led to war with China or worse—an atomic holocaust that history might have recorded as the world's last war. MacArthur's letter constituted a brazen challenge to the President's foreign policy and to presidential authority. A military commander had openly joined forces with the administration's foes. The Missourian resolutely took the inevitable step: he fired MacArthur from his commands in Japan and Korea and appointed General Ridgway in his place.

"I could do nothing else and still be President of the United States," Truman said later. "Even the Chiefs of Staff came to the conclusion that civilian control of the military was at stake and I didn't let it stay at stake very long."

Republicans, the China lobby and platoons of pundits poured out invective and abuse. MacArthur, meanwhile, returned to America for the first time in years and made a triumphal tour of San Francisco, Chicago, New York and Washington, basking in ovations which reached a climax with a melodramatic address before a joint session of Congress, but, in the end, the country recovered its equilibrium. Most thoughtful Americans understood and approved Truman's action. The MacArthur affair, however, only partially cleared the air of popular confusion over Far Eastern policy. That confusion would endure and would be projected into the 1960s.

The unification of Korea remained a political and diplomatic objective, but inasmuch as unification had been a political and not a military objective, the United Nations was able to accept a compromise that provided for communist withdrawal north of the thirty-eighth parallel. The principle was established that the U.S. would fight limited wars for limited objectives in order to avert the risk of world conflict, but in Vietnam, in the 1960s, the same dangers loomed as those that had prevailed in the Truman Era.

It was while Truman was still President that the United States began erecting a new "security system" in the Pacific. Mutual defense treaties were concluded in turn with the Philippines, Australia, New Zealand and Japan. The Security Treaty signed with the Japanese in San Francisco in the late summer of 1951 gave the United States the right to maintain land, sea and air bases on Japanese soil.

The creation of a broad anti-communist front resulted in a cease fire in Korea providing for mutual withdrawal of forces from the thirty-eighth parallel, but peace would not be restored until Peking agreed to an armistice during the Eisenhower Administration in 1953, ending a war that cost the United States 54,246 dead, 103,284 wounded and many billions of dollars.

It seems fairly evident from the foregoing that Truman was the principal architect of existing free world politico-military-economic barriers to Soviet imperialist expansion in Europe and to Sino-Russian ambitions in Asia. If he was right in pursuing the specific policies which resulted in the erection of those barriers—and who can say that, within the context of his epoch, he was not?—then he was unquestionably one of the heroes of our times.

11

Martin Luther King, Jr.

By POPPY CANNON

MARTIN LUTHER KING, JR.; born Atlanta, Georgia, January 15, 1929; son of Baptist minister Martin Luther King and Alberta Williams King; educated Atlanta public schools, Morehouse College, Crozer Theological Seminary, Boston University, University of Pennsylvania, Harvard; became pastor Dexter Avenue Baptist Church in Montgomery, Alabama, president Southern Christian Leadership Conference, co-pastor with his father Ebenezer Baptist Church, Atlanta; awarded Nobel Peace Prize 1964; assassinated Memphis, Tennessee, April 4, 1968.

Poppy Cannon is best known as the author of many cookbooks, a syndicated columnist on food and food editor of Ladies' Home Journal. But she is also the widow of the late Walter F. White, who devoted his life to his work with the National Association for the Advancement of Colored People and the fight against racial discrimination. As Mrs. White, she has written a column of general comment for the Amsterdam News, New York's oldest and most influential Negro newspaper. Dr. King was chosen as a hero for our times by members of the Overseas Press Club before he was murdered and, in connection with what she was to write about him, Poppy Cannon visited the Kings in At-

*lanta only a few weeks before that tragic event. "This was,"
according to a close friend of the family, "probably the last
full-dress interview in which he talked at length about himself and his ideas."*

THE DATE WAS APRIL 4; the year 1968; the time in New
York, about forty minutes after seven. In Memphis, it was
an hour earlier. I was working late trying to make a newspaper deadline. The phone rang.

"They've shot your friend. . . . Martin Luther King!"

"How bad is it?"

"In the jaw, they think. Turn on the radio."

I switched to an all-news station . . . to a convertible
sofa commercial, herring, an airline, a trip to Japan. Television was no better. The phone rang again.

"He's dead. The bulletin just came through. They've
killed him . . . a white man from across the street."

Strangely, my first reaction was blind rage. Against the
radio commercials that kept bleating, the Westerns, the
comedies on television with the bare, stark bulletins super-
imposed! I wanted details. My anger blazed against the
killer and killing, against the police, against the Establishment that let it—or made it—happen, against the whole
country with its violence, poverty, jailings, beatings,
napalm, Vietnam. First Kennedy murdered and now
King. . . .

Gradually, the fury changed to grief. But in the next
hours and days, when I heard of the riots in a hundred
towns and cities, the fires, the looting that became at times
a macabre carnival, ironically set off by the death of a man
dedicated to non-violence, I had a shamefaced understand-

ing. There was this need to hit out—if only to bloody your own fists against a stone wall.

Suddenly the airwaves and the TV channels were full of it, the first stunned, stuttering reports, clips from his speech at the rally of striking sanitation workers, the night before when he spoke of death and the Promised Land. "I've been on the mountain . . . I am not afraid. . . ."

In an unprecedented appearance that same evening, the President of the United States used a nation-wide hook-up to express shock and sorrow, and to plead for calm. Tributes and expressions of sympathy poured in from all over the world, except from the governors of southern states like his own native Georgia.

The nation and the world honored the young, black minister as no private citizen had ever been honored. For a few days, until after the funeral in Atlanta, most American flags flew at half mast as did the flag of the United Nations, a tribute never before accorded to a non-official.

Schools, colleges, libraries, banks, shops, factories and offices closed. Entertainment and sports events were postponed or canceled. The official big league baseball season did not begin as planned, nor were the Oscars passed out on schedule in Hollywood. The Motion Picture Academy ball and hundreds of others were called off.

In Atlanta, on Tuesday, the ninth of April, it was estimated that more than 150,000 people attended all or a part of the six-hour-long services which began a little after ten in the Ebenezer Baptist Church where Dr. King and his father had been co-pastors. The crowd formed a solid phalanx marching behind the rough farm cart drawn by two mules, to symbolize Dr. King's concern with the poor and the lowly. Dozens fainted in the hot sun in the street and by the flowering dogwoods, too, during the memorial speeches at Morehouse College. Thousands more followed him and his family to the segregated cemetery on the outskirts of the city, where in other times slaves found rest.

In their homes, watching television, millions of others were caught up on waves of emotion. All across our country and in Montreal, Rome, Paris, London, even in Moscow, there were memorials and marches. In the streets and in the churches, whites and blacks walked, sang, prayed together.

History will be a long time assaying the permanent effects of his life and his death. But already it seems clear that Martin Luther King Jr. was a man born to be a bridge, to bring people together, people of different minds and hearts and races. This had been made clear to me long before his death.

As the widow of Walter White, long-time executive secretary of the National Association for the Advancement of Colored People, I am asked from time to time to participate in various ceremonials. Not long before Dr. King was killed it was the dedication of a new branch of the NAACP in Indianapolis. Within minutes after my arrival in the city I was rushed to a series of interviews. Every one of the newspaper reporters and the radio and television interviewers flung at me, more or less sharply, this question: "What is your opinion of Martin Luther King? Has he hurt the civil rights cause by confusing it with his attacks on the war in Vietnam?"

Dr. King was at that moment embroiled in one of the most confused and bitter controversies of his career, sparked by his condemnation of the United States escalation of hostilities in Vietnam. Even white liberals and the spokesmen of powerful Negro organizations had expressed disagreement and chagrin. Many felt that he had done a disservice to the Negro cause, that he had, as some put it, "muddied the waters, interfered with progress in 'interracial' understanding."

The woman who faced me across the table at the television studio was kindly and earnest. She had explained to me before the program that she had been, for years, a great admirer of my husband, and had always taken an active role in civil rights. But, at this point, I gathered she was appalled. "What would your husband have thought?" she asked. "What is your own opinion about Dr. King's attitude on Vietnam?"

I said I had no way of knowing what Walter White would have thought or said except that I knew he hated war and violence in all its forms. As for me, I could not see how, as a man of God, Dr. King had any choice but to act and speak as he had spoken.

There was a queer stir in the studio. Everybody remained polite but not nearly as cordial as before.

Afterwards when I went downstairs I saw that the small delegation who had come with me to the studio had been joined by three young men, all tall and tieless, very dark and bare-throated. They had no black leather coats but they looked as if they should have been wearing them. They had been watching the television screen.

"You were fine," one said as he rose and towered over me. "You said just the right things. That's good," he went on, "because if you hadn't, we would have had to shoot you."

There was a small silence. Then he smiled, but briefly. The little group of doctors' wives and teachers, who had come to meet me at the airport gathered up their gloves and purses. We all laughed together. But nobody thought it was funny.

Then, and many times since then, I have thought that it was a portentous remark. For this young man was expressing not only black militancy but also the fact that Martin Luther King, exponent of non-violence, was a hero to him and his peers as well as to the more conservative people in the civil rights movement.

Dr. King had managed somehow to become this bridge not only between whites and blacks but between various factions of the Negro community. The leaders of the old-line, highly respected Urban League and the NAACP trusted him. So did young men like Stokely Carmichael and Floyd McKissick. He could speak not only for, but also to, the poor people in their own idiom and hold his own in the company of intellectuals.

My own special interest in Martin Luther King goes back a number of years, a few months after the death of my husband in 1955. The world was just beginning to hear about this catalyst, this leader and most eloquent spokesman of the bus boycott in Montgomery, Alabama, where the gentle seamstress, Rosa Parks, tired at the end of a long day, refused to give up her seat in the front of the bus. The black people of Montgomery joined with the Montgomery Improvement Association. They drove and formed car pools, they arranged for pickups in all parts of the city, they organized an elaborate web of transportation, they transformed a drugstore around the corner from the Capitol Building into campaign headquarters. But mostly they talked and they walked. "They walked their feet flat and their shoes into tatters." Eventually, with the virtually unknown young minister of the Dexter Avenue Baptist Church as the boycott leader, the bus companies of the "first city of the Confederacy" capitulated and Dr. King gained international recognition as the leader of the first great battle in what has come to be known as the Southern Negro Revolution.

About this time, an ambassador from Ceylon, one of the foremost Buddhist scholars of the East, was discussing with me the emergence of this young man in the South. "A new surge of leadership from a different quarter," he called it. "In many ways," he said, "it seems to be an extension, a revived continuance of the ideas of your husband."

I agreed that it was true.

"We have a theory amongst the Buddhists that a strong spirit like your husband's, one utterly dedicated to a cause, finds, after it has been freed from a mortal body, various ways to express itself, working not just through one but through many people. They choose instruments that are compatible. Have you ever thought of that?" He smiled and I had the feeling that he was only partially serious. But the idea stayed with me. I began reading about Dr. King with a new feeling.

In many ways Dr. Martin Luther King Jr. "was compatible" with Walter White though he did not know him well. His father, Martin Luther King Sr., was a friend and contemporary. Years later he told me he had never had a real conversation with Walter but knew him only through his reputation and books. Yet they had many of the same patterns of thought and even of speech. They belonged to a group practically unknown and completely ignored by the white world. This is the group whose white counterparts are known as the backbone of American civilization. They are the middle class. Some are doctors, lawyers, dentists, teachers, civil servants; others are businessmen, real estate agents, insurance salesmen and executives. They are not the hungry, nor the cold or unlettered. Their children go regularly to schools. Many like the Kings and Whites have been graduating from colleges for generations. There are not many really wealthy families amongst this group but they are solid citizens, thrifty, well off.

Like Walter White, King was an intellectual, a man of elegance, with a knowledge of and taste for good food, good clothes, good talk but precious little time to enjoy them and not one jot of interest in building a life around them. In both, the dedication was complete, soul-deep and lifelong. Their backgrounds were the same. They came from the same neighborhoods, from the same kind of families—gentle, cultured people who gave their children just enough but not too much of the world's goods plus great love and strict upbringing.

There was more money in the King household. The family had made some wise investments, mostly in real estate. Walter White's father, in spite of his training at Atlanta University, was a postman. Martin Luther King's father is, and his grandfather was, a highly respected Baptist minister.

Contrary to the popular notion, Martin Luther King was not a ragged little boy from a backwoods cabin or the cotton fields Down South. His maternal grandfather, Dr. A. D. Williams, was pastor of the same large and well-heeled Ebenezer Baptist Church, which his father inherited and over which he himself eventually presided.

It is true that he was once, in accordance with the great American tradition, a newsboy. He delivered newspapers—in the South they call it "throwing papers." But it was because he wanted rather than needed to earn pocket money. He likes to tell the story of the neighborhood hassle that resulted when he refused to "throw" the paper on the doorstep of a local dentist who insulted him. Despite his boycott of the dentist, and even at this early age, Martin Luther King had a penchant for success. He became at twelve the main organizer, the tactical boss, of all the newspaper "throwers" in his section of the city.

In his personal as well as in his spiritual and philosophical development he always displayed an unusual ability to build bridges between the past and the present, between the old and the new. He did not break with the past. Neither was he held back by it. He stood on top of it—on the shoulders of the giants. And he went on from where they stopped.

Freely he admitted that he was shaped by many influences and many persons. Perhaps the earliest and one of the strongest influences was his father. From his father he learned to be strong, to be shrewd. For all his gentleness, he was shrewd. He learned also to be a battler.

From his mother, he learned gentleness and tact, if not patience.

The Christian teachings of Jesus were not amongst his earliest conscious influences though he was brought up in a deeply religious, even fundamentalist, atmosphere. As a boy, he rebelled against religion. For a time he was an agnostic, perhaps even an atheist. He had no thought of following in his grandfather's and his father's footsteps.

When he entered Morehouse College at the age of fifteen, he expected to be a doctor. A year or so later, his ambition switched to law. Not until the summer of his junior year, when he worked (once again from choice, not necessity) in the tobacco fields of Connecticut, did he realize that his calling had to be the ministry. Already the teachings of Mahatma Gandhi had begun to shape his thinking. He was intrigued and enthralled by Thoreau, the quiet philosopher of Walden. Later, when he studied theology at Crozer Seminary in Chester, Pennsylvania, and received his Ph.D. from Boston University and his Doctor of Divinity degree from the Chicago Theological Seminary, he found a special appeal in the works of the Biblical prophets Amos, Isaiah, Jeremiah and Micah, "for their emphasis was not on ceremonial but on social justice in religion."

Always before, in the hundred-year struggle of the American Negro for full citizenship, the church, both black and white, has stayed in the background of the struggle. Some few prelates have spoken up, but for the most part America remained, and in many places still remains, "most segregated at eleven o'clock on a Sunday morning."

Martin Luther King may be credited with initiating a great change amongst churchmen and churchgoers. The change has been less obvious in the white community. In the Negro churches and especially in Southern Negro churches, it has been revolutionary. Passivity had no place in the nature of this man. Militancy did not disturb Dr. King, but violence offended him in all its forms. He was perturbed but not at all moved by the fact that violence has become a stylish concept among young intellectuals of both races. He admitted that it is one of the great debates of history whether good ends can be achieved by bad or hurtful means. "You can't separate the two," he said. "The end is pre-existent in the means. Destructive methods cannot bring about a constructive conclusion."

One day, in his office on Auburn Street—Sweet Auburn, it used to be called, the heart of Atlanta's Negro ghetto— he mused upon these matters. "The means is the seed," he said, "and the end is the tree; they cannot be separated.

Immoral actions have," he admitted, "sometimes brought about temporary victories. But real peace cannot be won through war or through violence. Inevitably violence begets more violence, war begets more war."

He did not categorically condemn Black Power and its advocates. "There are positives in Black Power," he said. "Black Power if properly defined and soberly used can be a prized tool. Black Power can provide spokesmen."

Unlike Walter White, who knew he must be committed to the civil rights fight when, at the age of twelve, he stood with his gentle father in the front room, gun in hand, ready to fight off a rampaging white mob in an Atlanta race riot, Martin Luther King experienced no such childhood traumas. One incident, however, rankled for years. He was a member of the Booker T. Washington High School Debating Society and went with his team to Dublin, Georgia, to an oratorical contest, a statewide tourney at which he won a prize. Flushed with success and for the moment forgetting about the *mores* of Georgia, all took seats toward the front of the bus. There was the inevitable trouble. "At first," said Dr. King, "I refused to go to the back of the bus. The teacher pleaded with me. She said it would be advisable. But I couldn't go back. I could never be silent or neutral. I had to stand all the way to Atlanta. It was late at night and I was tired, but that wasn't the point. It was the humiliation. Suddenly I realized you don't count, you're nobody."

Certainly his was, in this case, a minor wound, but as he told the story the prickles went up and down my spine. For Martin Luther King was a great actor. Certainly he thrived on adulation. He had a genius for making headlines but he was not an intentional nor a professional charmer. He did not go out of his way to enthrall everyone he met. He was willing to accept criticism, calumny and abuse, even from those who were formerly on his side, when convinced he was doing the right thing.

Nobody in all his career was ever able to bribe him—certainly not with money or power or position or even a Cabinet post. As one of his parishioners put it, "They can't bribe him with either love or with praise. They gave him the Nobel Prize for peace but even that didn't make him stand still. Even if the President asks him to the White House, it makes him no matter."

One day in his office, I repeated this comment to Dr. King. His eyes twinkled but his mouth was firm. He quoted someone, I was not quite sure whom, maybe himself, "Caution asks, is it safe? Expediency asks, is it politic? Vanity asks, is it popular? But conscience asks, is it right?"

To those who might question Dr. King's lack of gratitude to President Lyndon Johnson who he admitted had done more for civil rights than any other President in history, Dr. King answered sadly, "The Great Society was the first casualty of the war in Vietnam." And although his lifelong interest was in the field of improving the lot of the Afro-Americans, Dr. King felt he must involve himself in every possible protest against war. "What is the point," he asked, "of working for equality and integration unless you work to insure at the same time the survival of a world in which to integrate?"

Integration, the concept to which leaders like my husband had devoted their lives, has become a naughty word in some circles, both black and white. Segregationists are flourishing amongst the extremists on both sides of the color line. But, in Dr. King's philosophy, there was room for segregation (strictly voluntary segregation) as well as integration. "I belong," he said, "to the Both-And school.

Temporary and voluntary segregation may be a way-station in the march toward equality. With good conscience one can work for better schools in the ghettos and at the same time work and march and pray for open housing which is the only possible way to eliminate ghettos."

I happened to be in Atlanta on the afternoon when the ladies of the West Hunter Street Baptist Church arranged a reception rally for Dr. King and their pastor, Dr. Ralph Abernathy, to celebrate one of their homecomings from jail. Dr. Abernathy, close and longtime colleague of Dr. King, who succeeded him as head of the Southern Christian Leadership Conference after his death, was one of five clergymen who shared a prison dormitory in Bessemer, Alabama, and later a cell in Birmingham during a five-day term.

Within minutes after their arrival in the Atlanta airport, the men of God were rushed to the rally in the parish house of the church. With a fine sense of drama both ministers appeared in rough worn clothes, the uniform of the "Movement." They wore them with considerable flair. Over his blue denim shirt Dr. Abernathy had a soft beige cashmere sweater, casual but really elegant. Dr. King stood so straight and proud that his brass-buttoned denim jacket looked almost military.

The parish room was crowded. To one side, there was a table covered with a lace cloth and decorated with flowers, candles, trays of sandwiches and fancy little cakes. In the audience was a large group of college and university students, white and black, all assiduously taking notes. Considering the drama of the occasion, there seemed to me to be a dearth of television, radio and newspaper reporters.

"Because they don't rave, shout, and rant, Abernathy and King are not considered such big news right now," said one young man with an undertone of rancor in his voice. "It's the wild ones that get the exposure. The crazier they talk, the more people listen to them."

Yet the quiet voice of Dr. Abernathy held not a trace of malice as he spoke about the days spent in the jail at Bessemer, known as the heart of the Ku Klux Klan country. The local sheriff and the jailer were not bad men, he said. "We prayed to God to open their hearts." He described how, at one point before they left to finish their terms in Birmingham, all five of the prisoners and their jailers knelt in a circle and sang, "What a fellowship . . . in the Lord."

"The jailer took the lead; he was first tenor."

The respect for each other and the cooperation between the authorities and the prisoners made an unusual story which was completely ignored by the Southern press and, as a matter of fact, by all the press.

For Dr. King, at 38, it was his nineteenth jailing. "We know it will not be the last," he said. But it was!

The Nobel Peace Prize winner remained completely committed to the course that he had chosen, "I will rot in jail before I make a butchery of my conscience. No matter how old you get to be, you are walking dead when you refuse to stand up for right." *Right,* he admitted, is, unfortunately, not always the same as *lawful:* "Everything that Hitler did to the Jews in Nazi Germany was done under the law. It was legal—because Hitler made the laws."

Repeatedly Dr. King was tagged in conservative circles with the label of extremist. Those on the other end of the seesaw named him, with more or less venom, Dr. Lawd or L.L.J. for "Little Lord Jesus."

To many of the young people, white and black, who took part in the voter registration drive during the bleak summer of 1965, a campaign that culminated in hundreds of crimes of violence, reported and unreported, and in the murder of three young civil rights workers, a Unitarian minister from Boston and a Detroit housewife, the appearance of Dr. King upon the scene was not always considered an unmixed blessing.

Veterans of that fevered summer recall a bit of doggerel on the subject:

> *De Lawd he come, he seek, he spoke,*
> *De Lawd he go . . .*
> *We get our asses broke.*

Nevertheless it is true, and Dr. King said it himself, that he stood between two opposing forces in the Negro community. "One is a force of complacency made up of Negroes who, as a result of long years of oppression, have been so completely drained of self-respect and a sense of 'somebodiness' that they have adjusted to segregation, and a few Negroes in the middle class who, because of a degree of academic and economic security, and because at points they profit from segregation, have unconsciously become insensitive to the problems of the masses.

"The other force is one of bitterness and hatred . . . it is made up of people who have absolutely repudiated Christianity and have concluded that the white man is an incurable devil. . . . I have tried to stand between these two forces . . ."

He went on to say that "if our white brothers dismiss, as 'rabble rousers' and 'outside agitators,' those of us who are working through the channels of non-violent efforts, millions of Negroes, out of frustration and despair, will seek solace and security in black nationalist ideologies, a development that will lead inevitably to a frightening racial nightmare."

The time was 1964. The place was City Hall in Manhattan, a large reception hall adjoining the mayor's office. The room was crowded to the doors with friends, press, city officials gathered to honor the winner of the Nobel Prize for Peace.

New York accorded to Martin Luther King Jr. a modest hero's welcome upon his return from Sweden where he was named Nobel Peace Prize laureate. His nomination for the coveted award came "because he had succeeded in keeping his followers to the principles of non-violence." They had added (these eight august members of the Swedish Parliament who made up the jury) "that without King's confirmed effectiveness, demonstrations and marchers could easily have become violent and ended in the spilling of blood." For some reason unexplained the Nobel Committee did not, as was usual, announce the basis for the award, which is supposed to be given annually "to the person who has done the most for the furtherance of brotherhood among men and the abolition or reduction of standing armies and for the extension of these purposes."

Seated on the elegantly raised platform were the four Kings—father and son, mother and daughter-in-law. The resemblance between them was striking. The senior Mrs. King had never been a great beauty like Coretta King, who is a singer, talented as well as lovely, but they have the same build, they move in the same way. The shape of the head, the cut of the chin is hauntingly similar. I spoke of this to the Harlem banker who was sitting beside me. "It is a good sign," he said, "when a man picks a wife who looks like his mother or a beloved sister. It shows that he is at peace with his own background."

The speakers that day mentioned that Dr. King was the youngest person ever to receive the Nobel award since it was started in 1895, the third Negro, the twelfth American.

The man beside me moved uneasily in his chair, "Now that King has his crown, I wonder. Will it stop him? Will it keep him quiet? Will he be afraid to risk his dignity?"

Within a few months all these questions were answered. The answer in every case was no. He was a King who accepted the Nobel crown with all becoming modesty and a fair show of appreciation. Then he wore it to work!

The "Wall of Fame" which Coretta King arranged in their home has become unbelievably crowded with hundreds of citations, awards, plaques and medals, honorary degrees by the dozen. *Time* magazine named him in 1963 as Man of the Year, an honor accorded to only one other black man, the Emperor Haile Selassie of Ethiopia in 1927.

Many accused Dr. King and his followers of breaking the law. He admitted that it is a legitimate concern. "Since we so diligently urge people to obey the Supreme Court's decision of 1954 outlawing segregation in the public schools, it is rather strange and paradoxical to find us consciously breaking laws."

Nevertheless he believed that sit-ins, pray-ins, lobby-ins, marches, non-violent demonstrations of many kinds are defensible and valuable.

"One may well ask how can you advocate breaking some laws and obeying others. Because," he contended, "there are, St. Augustine has said, just and unjust laws."

"For instance," he wrote in a famous letter from jail, "I was arrested on Friday on a charge of parading without a permit. Now there is nothing wrong with an ordinance which requires a permit for a parade but when the ordinance is used to preserve segregation and to deny citizens the First Amendment privilege of peaceful assembly and peaceful protest, then it becomes unjust . . .

"One who breaks an unjust law must do it *openly, lovingly,* not hatefully as the white mothers did in New Orleans when they were seen on television screaming nigger, nigger, nigger. . . . I submit that an individual who breaks the law that consience tells him is unjust and willingly accepts the penalty by staying in jail to arouse the conscience of the community . . . is in reality expressing the very highest respect for law."

Many times I had heard Walter White express his impatience with what he sometimes called the "lily-livered liberals, the so-called moderates who," as he expressed it, "sit on the fence with their legs firmly planted in mid-air." On several occasions he admitted, "I would rather take my chances with the out-and-out segregationist. With him at least you know where you are."

Martin Luther King put it another way. "I must confess," he wrote, "that over the last few years, I have been gravely disappointed with the white moderate. I have almost reached the regrettable conclusion that the Negro's great stumbling block in the stride toward freedom is not the White Citizens' Council or the Ku Klux Klanners, but the white moderate who is more devoted to order than to justice."

Who knows what importance historians writing of the Twentieth Century will give to the march on Washington which took place at the end of one summer, on August 28, 1963. Not since the crusades of the Middle Ages had there been such an outpouring of people led by the force of an idea. At least a quarter of a million—more than half of them white—came by car and bus, by train and plane into the capital city. There was an incredible dignity about them, a quiet, solid pride as they came together to celebrate the anniversary of the signing of the Emancipation Proclamation in that same city one hundred years before.

Martin Luther King spoke that afternoon at the foot of the Lincoln Memorial. In a brief speech broadcast and televised across the world, he called it "the greatest demonstration for freedom in the history of the nation."

Certainly now it seems possible that this speech may rank with the Gettysburg address of Abraham Lincoln as one of the most prized documents of our nation. In the soft, heart-tugging, well-tutored, velvety tones of a Baptist preacher, touched ever so slightly with the blur of his native South, he spoke of the hundred years that had passed. "The Negro lives," he said, "on a lonely island of poverty in the midst of a vast ocean of material prosperity . . ."

At times he spoke in everyday language.

"In a sense we've come to our nation's capital to cash a check. When the architects of our Republic wrote the magnificent words of the Constitution and the Declaration of Independence they were signing a promissory note . . . Instead of honoring this sacred obligation, America has given the Negro people a bad check, a check which has come back marked, 'insufficient funds.' "

Then again, he invoked lofty images. "The whirlwinds of revolt," he warned, "will continue to shake the foundations of our nation until the bright day of justice emerges. . . . Let us not seek to satisfy our thirst for freedom by drinking from the cup of bitterness and hatred."

He acknowledged the presence of so many thousands of white participants. "The marvelous new militancy which has engulfed the Negro community must not lead us to distrust all white people, for many of our white brothers, as evidenced by their presence here today, have come to realize that their destiny is tied up with our destiny . . .

"We cannot walk alone . . ."

A few moments later, he spoke the words that may well be preserved amongst the deathless sentences of our age, "I have a dream . . ."

Dr. King later admitted with disarming frankness that it was not the first time he had used this expression.

Half a dozen years before he had on one occasion made the remark, "Last night in the kitchen of my home, I had a vision . . ." This was not, at the time, a fortunate choice of words. A newspaper columnist pounced upon it. Dr. King was ribbed unmercifully about his "vision in the kitchen."

Many months later, as he recalled it, in the midst of the voter registration drive in Albany, Georgia, there was an evening when his audience seemed tired, discouraged, apathetic. He had a feeling that he could not get through to them. He stopped talking about the problems of the moment. He dropped his voice. His eyes looked off, as if to far places.

Then he began (and his audience was electrified as they were to be a few years afterwards in Washington), "I have a dream . . . That one day on the red hills of Georgia, sons of former slaves and the sons of former slave-owners will be able to sit down together at the table of brotherhood. I have a dream that one day even the state of Mississippi, a state sweltering with the heat of injustice, sweltering with the heat of oppression, will be transformed into an oasis of freedom and justice.

"I have a dream that my four children will one day live in a nation where they will not be judged by the color of their skin but by the content of their character. I have a dream . . . I have a dream that one day in Alabama, with its vicious racists, with its governor having his lips dripping with the words of interposition and nullification, one day right there in Alabama little black boys and black girls will be able to join hands with little white boys and white girls as sisters and brothers."

To an extraordinary degree he helped to make these visions real. There are those who say that, through his death by assassination at the age of 39, he may have done more to awaken the conscience of America than if, in the normal course of events, he had lived forty years longer.

Of one thing there is no doubt. Martin Luther King Jr. brought to black people a new pride and gave to his country a new stature in the eyes of the world.

12

Dag Hammarskjöld

By BURNET HERSHEY

DAG HJALMAR AGNE KARL HAMMARSKJÖLD; born Jönköping, Sweden, July 29, 1905; son of Swedish World War I premier Hjalmar Hammarskjöld; educated Uppsala University and University of Stockholm; successively teacher of political science Stockholm, secretary Bank of Sweden, chairman Bank of Sweden, Undersecretary of Finance, chief delegate to Organization for European Economic Cooperation and vice chairman executive committee, assistant foreign minister, deputy foreign minister, chairman Swedish delegation United Nations General Assembly, secretary general United Nations; died in airplane crash near Ndola, Northern Rhodesia, September 18, 1961; posthumously awarded Nobel Peace Prize for 1961.

Burnet Hershey, a founder of the Overseas Press Club, has been a foreign correspondent since 1917. He covered Henry Ford's effort to end World War I with his "Peace Ship" expedition, served as a correspondent with the French and Belgian armies as well as with the German armies on the Eastern front, and was the youngest correspondent at the Versailles peace conference after the war. During World War II, he wrote for the New York Post and Liberty from Great Britain, North Africa, France and occupied Germany. His friendship with Dag Hammarskjöld began at one

*of the thirty-eight international conferences he has covered.
He published a biography of Hammarskjöld in 1961.*

WHEN CARLYLE SAID, "History is the essence of innumerable biographies," he might well have been writing of a man like the late Dag Hammarskjöld whose biographies have become a distillation of all the perils and anxieties of our own chapter of history.

It has happened to most of the great actors on the world's stage that their posthumous fame has undergone many vicissitudes. Not Hammarskjöld's, whose image has remained intact and whose techniques in the art of quiet diplomacy (quiet but not invisible) are sorely missed by a world in turmoil. It is a belief widely held that if Dag were alive and at his helm in the United Nations' glass house in New York, peace would not be in such jeopardy.

In the brief compass of this sketch and with even the most merciless economy of compression it is difficult to tell the Hammarskjöld story, particularly as it relates to the procession of crisis after crisis, and the manner in which he brought his peace-keeping talents into play. In a world retching from smoke-inhalation from dozens of brush-fire wars and teeter-tottering on the edge of greater doom, this quiet man of rugged determination was able to exercise a role unique in all history: the use of power and persuasion because he represented no personal ambition, no government, no special interest. Because of its purely international character, his UN administration thus became a symbol of the world's conscience. So the influence of this man, his short life and his dramatic death has flowed out and on beyond the men and women he worked with, beyond the borders of the East River to those who never knew him.

It is said that when the subject is complicated, try drawing a simple picture.

Even to this author, whose researches here and in Sweden resulted in the biography *Soldier of Peace,* published in 1961 after his death, Hammarskjöld cannot be easily understood or explained. At best, one might try to "stick figure" the astonishing variety of his being: scholar, statesman, poet, translator, mystical theologist-philosopher, martyr, naturalist outdoorsman, skilled mountaineer, moody esthete, buoyant friend.

So, we start this portrait by drawing the crown of Dag, the baby. His mother was the beautiful Agnes Almquist Hammarskjöld, wife of Hjalmar Hammarskjöld, top ranking public servant in international law and President of the Gota Court Advisors, the Jönköping Court of Appeal in south central Sweden; and Minister of Religion in Prime Minister Christian Lundeberg's cabinet.

Dag's mother knew, on the stormy summer evening of July 29, 1905, that her fourth child, after a barren period of five years, would be born that evening because the familiar pains of imminent childbirth were very much upon her. As she lay attended by her private physician in her elegant bed inside their lakeside residence in Villa Liljelholmen, province of Smaaland, the doctor noted that her severe labor pains were causing her to lose consciousness. But, before she lapsed into a faint, she managed to gasp, "Please, God, we already have three wonderful boys; it must be a *girl!"*

The lovely Mrs. Hammarskjöld never truly accepted the biological fact that the final offspring she was to produce— so perfectly male and looking like a fair blue-eyed angel—

was indeed a boy and not a girl. So obsessed was she for the need to have a child who "looked just like me"—as her adoring husband had wished—that the family albums alone attest what Dag had to endure as his mother's "boy."

Mrs. Hammarskjöld was in her forties when her youngest son was born and her fertile child-bearing period was ebbing to its normal close. She was unable to reconcile herself to the fact that there was no little picture-postcard-of-herself female in the family. Little Dag not only had his golden hair painstakingly coiffed in long curls, but the obedient little boy wore girl's clothes for quite some time after his diaper and toddler stage.

Sven Stolpe, who was closely associated with Dag in his youth, observed in an essay he wrote about him that outwardly "Dag was a markedly virile person, entirely free from feminine traits of character (once his curls and dainty doll clothes were gone), yet he had no difficulty in accepting his mother's kindly despotism . . . he devotedly loved his exacting mother."

While she often neglected her other three sons, author Sten Soderberg, who made an authoritative study of all the Hammarskjölds, wrote, "Dag was his mother's gentleman-in-waiting, her page, her faithful and considerable attendant."

Throughout his life, Dag never married and apparently —according to those who knew him most intimately—he never had any romantic or sustained relationship with a woman. Inside the homes he maintained when he was Secretary General of the United Nations, his companion-aides were male.

Once, he compared himself to a "Catholic priest who renounces marriage in order to give his love to all." He lived intensively in his work, was severely self-disciplined;

made and kept friends with a great loyalty and comradeship. He considered being detached from emotional entanglements "the innermost reality of life."

Yet many women, knowing it unlikely Hammarsköld would ever be drawn to the altar, were swift to be enamored of him. His commanding eyes were so clear and provokingly unspoken in their thoughts: his smile was surprisingly mischievous looking; he was so capable in everything he undertook; his leadership and dependability so evident, all very appealing traits for a woman seeking a substantial man to "honor and protect" her. It is no wonder they desired him.

It was well known to members of the United Nations press corps that scores of lady delegates and diplomats and, in particular, one of the best-known women news commentators, were—some transitorily, and the newsgal forever—hopelessly in love with him. When the stunning news of his sudden death in a plane crash was received in the world organization, close friends of this fine journalist feared the loss of her idol would lead to her serious collapse, but she stoically remained on the job, believing undoubtedly that in this way she could continue still to serve him, and that this is what he would have admired. Today, in memorials to Dag, and whenever his name crops up, which is still often, she remains one of his most glowing spokesmen.

More positively one may speak of Dag's perpetually virile and brilliantly productive intellectuality. Despite what are often the disadvantages of an over-indulged childhood and youth (as a student he lived in aristocratic surroundings in Vasa Castle instead of a room on the Uppsala University campus and hadn't the conditioning of having overcome hardships), the drive to serve, to be useful, to taste every wonder in life was ceaselessly and restlessly inherent within him.

He was a member of postwar Europe's "transient generation," realizing fully the terrible price his own father and other fathers had paid for what is mockingly known as "victory" in World War I—or "victory" in any war, for that matter. The young man, Dag, who was doubly stimulated by living in an intellectual climate at home as well as at the University, would often ask his father, then the Prime Minister, for answers to problems in international relations and he'd be able to receive answers few other fathers could give.

His own questions were like those of most of his other college friends. "Is it not possible that the world has learned its lesson? Is there nothing that can be done to see to it that no such crimes shall ever happen again? Is not all the suffering and destruction a crushing indictment of the military epoch out of which no one has really emerged victorious?"

When Dag was only twenty-two, and still a student, he relished what it was like to take part in public affairs by being appointed First Secretary of Uppland's three hundredth anniversary celebration. He took care of all the complicated public arrangements, made speeches and got hit with the "bug" of enjoying public exposure and involvement.

There is a myth that Dag was self-effacing, shy and inhibited. He may have been shy about the initial step of coming forward—for fear of not winning out, perhaps—but he always forced himself forward, and his ego, his self-belief, his ambitious need for meaningful and constructive power, was always big.

After earning a law degree in England at Cambridge in

1930, he was rewarded with an unexpected appointment as Secretary of the Unemployment Insurance Plan, a great plum for such a young man of twenty-five. And this is when Dag's own meteoric career in government began.

Dag Hammarskjöld became "Doctor Hammarskjöld" by virtue of earning a Ph.D. in economics with a thesis that earned him a reputation as a financial wizard. It carried the jaw-breaking title of *Konjunkurspridningen, A Theoretical and Historical Survey of Market Trends*. By then he was an assistant professor at the University of Stockholm and almost overnight achieved recognition from Sweden's top economic theorists.

The first important man aware of Hammarskjöld's gift for understanding finance was Ernst Wigforss, a former Minister of Finance, who approached Hammarskjöld to head a committee being formed to combat Sweden's serious unemployment problem. In his usual painstaking manner, Dag's exhaustive survey of the unemployment picture resulted in recommendations summed up as "bafflingly technical, but the practical measures he advanced kept unemployment lower in Sweden than in most European countries." Thus, he became established as one of the most prominent figures in the Swedish financial world.

It is well to reflect on the diverse and unexpected gifts of this man that most people as literary as he, as dreamy and poetic, as much interested in the arts, in the great outdoors, run like the devil from a subject such as economics or mathematics. Not so Dag, who, it seemed, was master of many traits and slack at none.

His move up the ladder in public service soared with his configurations with mathematical googolplexes. At thirty-one, he was made Permanent Secretary to the Ministry of

Finance and then, simultaneously, Chairman of the Riks-bank, the first man ever to hold both posts at once.

At the end of World War II, after he had been trans-ferred to the Foreign Office as under-secretary in charge of financial affairs, his abilities were well noted and remem-bered among the nations which were later to sponsor his rise in the UN.

During the Paris conference of the Organization for European Economic Cooperation, all the delegates were astounded at his gigantic capacity for work and his stub-bornness about unlocking the key to the most difficult prob-lems. It was in this atmosphere of tension, debates and handwringings that those at the Paris conference recog-nized Dag was no mere machine but a gifted diplomat who won his points and scored with the highest level of finesse. In succession came his appointment as Sweden's Deputy Foreign Minister, Vice Chairman of the Swedish Delega-tion to the UN in 1951, Chairman in 1952. He was just a step away from his martyred destiny as highest peace mediator to the United Nations.

After the Soviets forced his fellow Scandinavian, Trygve Lie, the UN's first Secretary General, to resign on Novem-ber 10, 1952, Dag was taking a boulevard stroll in Sweden when he was cornered by newsmen and told that informa-tion from New York confirmed he had been nominated by the French and unanimously endorsed by members of the Security Council to become the next Secretary General. He thought they were trying to create news with a trial balloon, so he said: "I am amused, but not interested."

However, he did bother to query New York about the suspected "hoax." Who knows what flood of excitement and challenge coursed through him when he realized that he was indeed chosen to enter the race for the job of assuming the overwhelming responsibility as the world's leading manager of the peace?

Dag's fabulous stamina became legendary when he succeeded Lie as Secretary General of the UN in 1953, when he was forty-eight. His first self-assigned orientation was to tell his first executive assistant, Andrew Cordier, that he wished to meet every UN employee in the entire structure which comprises the dramatic-looking world peace edifice.

"But," said Cordier, in disbelief, "we have about four thousand employees. You don't mean you want to meet every clerical worker as well as every department head, do you?"

"I mean precisely that," Hammarsköld said.

"But that will take at least two months, Mr. Secretary."

"No, it won't. Let's just approach it floor by floor. And let's begin today."

That is exactly what happened. Hammarskjöld shook hands with every single one of the four thousand employees, saying, "I am here to serve you all." This unique feat in employer-employee relations was finished at the end of fourteen days. And Dag had made four thousand new, loyal friends who would stick fast by him to the shattering last.

The Secretary General began his day at an early breakfast, diligently taking painstaking review of at least four major newspapers and circling items which bore upon decisions he might have to make during the day. At especially critical times, such as the Suez crisis, he would sleep on a sofa bed in the small apartment adjoining his office.

Late in December of 1956, after months of strife which had the United Nations Emergency Force maintaining free passage through the Suez canal, Hammarskjöld's housekeeper came up to his breakfast table and spoke almost apologetically: "Please excuse me, Mr. Hammarskjöld, but you have had no rest for weeks. You must at least take a Christmas holiday."

"Why, of course," agreed the Secretary General. He spent Christmas in Suez, sharing the Yuletide celebrations with the men who could not go home that year—the troops of the UNEF who had brought an interval of peace on earth to men of goodwill. To them and to the world, "General Hammarskjöld" had unquestionably averted war.

There were many exciting roles the Secretary General played, as he indefatigably encircled the globe, in such dramas as the liberation of the American flyers from Red China and the desperate intervention to stave off chaos in the rain forest of the Congo. But the business of quenching global fires was only one part of his monumental job. The less glamorous side—the paper-work side—was unpublicized to the general public.

Each morning, Hammarskjöld's desk was piled with letters and documents noting contacts with some two and a half billion clients, the entire population of the world.

In many respects, he was really the chief executive of the world. Thus, as "president" of the world, he guided the machinery of a sprawling global operation. He dealt with a multiplicity of agencies with headquarters in a dozen world capitals, and branches and subdivisions in the most farflung and isolated spots of the earth. UN missions are found in about 110 countries, to say nothing of the thirty UN information centers in as many capitals. This vast apparatus is charged with bettering mankind's condition in every single walk of life.

During any typical week at the UN, Hammarskjöld was directly involved in answering a multitude of questions such as these: How can a program of schoolroom inoculation against cholera be expedited in Saudi Arabia? Should funds be allocated for a long-range study of the swollen shoot blight which affects cocoa trees? Should there be a literacy requirement for voters in Ruanda-Urundi? What is the potential agricultural yield from a proposed dam and hydroelectric plant on the Niger River? Can several thousand refugees be resettled in Australia? How can a program of recruiting student nurses in South Vietnam be stepped up? (Yes, we were involved in Vietnam even back then.) Should portable film units be used for adult education in Pakistan?

These are only a handful of the hundreds of questions Hammarskjöld handled every week, each answer requiring plodding work with the particular UN agency involved in the problem. It required his presence at endless conferences; it demanded he read report after voluminous report. And all of these matters, removed from international politics, were dear to the "priest" heart in Hammarskjöld. They were that side of the UN operation which was dedicated to the health and the well-being of individuals, to life, liberty, and the pursuit of happiness. These were the lesser known of his efforts at the UN but to him the work was a "restorative" if what came out of it meant more food for the hungry, better education for the unschooled, rehabilitation for the handicapped or improved efficiency for the economies of the infant countries.

In the precious few hours away from his daily labors, at his eight-room duplex Park Avenue apartment in Manhattan, how did the man of perpetual motion refresh himself, relax?

Regardless of what crisis may have been hovering over the UN, Hammarskjöld would and could get away from it all with four main passions of his life: reading, listening to music, translating the works of revered authors, communing with nature. Hammarskjöld said he was habituated to reading about three hours each night, and he called the Bible, Shakespeare and *Don Quixote* indispensable. But he also roamed as far afield as the "beat" author, Jack Kerouac, and, as a member of the Nobel Prize Committee, he conscientiously read every single literary work submitted for consideration. His favorite authors were T. S. Eliot, James Joyce, Thomas Wolfe, Joseph Conrad, Marcel Proust, Thomas Mann and St. John Perse, the latter occupying a special niche in his admiration because he gave up a diplomatic career for poetry!

In 1960, Hammarskjöld translated Perse's *Chronicles* from the French into Swedish. "Isn't it amazing," a friend commented, "that the man who had the Congo on his hands in August, and Khrushchev on his back in October, could still find rest and pleasure in polishing a manuscript of poetry before sending it home to Sweden for publication? Surely this is one of his many secret weapons."

Though Hammarskjöld never studied any musical instrument formally, listening to music played a much more important part in his life than most people realized. Like the disciplined and undemonstrative type he was himself, he preferred the intricate and subtle fugues of Bach and Scarlatti to the work of more thundering composers such as Wagner and Berlioz. He was also especially fond of Beethoven's Ninth Symphony and established it as a "must" at the regularly held UN Day concerts.

Hammarskjöld's personal circle of friends included mostly people in music and the arts rather than in diplomacy. Those invited to his small informal dinners at his home in Manhattan and his country retreat in Brewster,

New York, included Leonard Bernstein, Pablo Casals, Fritz Kreisler, Alfred H. Barr, John Steinbeck and their wives. Hammarskjöld liked to give his cook a night off on these occasions and himself concoct exotic and elaborate variations on the smorgasbord theme.

Sedentary or physically vital, young or old, his guests at Brewster were also always in for hours of outdoors hiking in the nearby woods, day or night. If the guests were unanimous that *they* were not in the mood, he'd march out good naturedly alone. He could not live, he often said, without feasting his eyes on nature's beauty, without moving his body and employing its rhythms and strength.

Within the tight and small circle of his friends here and those he cherished back home in Sweden and in other parts of the world, Hammarskjöld—much as he wished to be "emotionally detached to achieve the real reality"—was once described by a British correspondent as being "positively maudlin" about his sentimental attachments to his friends. He never failed to remember a birthday, anniversary or other personal occasion. A sick friend would always get an encouraging note; an old schoolmate would be remembered with a couple of tickets for the meeting of the Swedish Academy. It was always a wonder how he found time for this unfailing thoughtfulness.

For all his capacity for friendship, for all the world adulation of his brilliant statesmanship, Hammarskjöld suffered frequent attacks of agonized loneliness, as we know from his self-directed posthumously published autobiographical book, *Markings,* which he called "a sort of white book concerning my negotiations with myself and with God."

In one of his despairings over the almost physical toll that loneliness can take, he wrote: "Loneliness is not the sickness unto death. No, but can it be endured except by death? And does it not become the harder to bear the closer one comes to death?"

Hammarskjöld's love affair with death and his love affair with life ceased in the summer's end of a stormy world on September 17, 1961, in central Africa, while he was on one of his innumerable peace missions.

He was flying from Léopoldville to Ndola, scheduled for Congo truce talks with President Moise Tshombe of Katanga in hopes of arranging a cease-fire between United Nations police forces and Tshombe's rebels.

Tshombe had persistently scorned the UN since he had taken over as "strong man." Nevertheless, on September 18, he had consented to talk peace with Hammarskjöld and had voiced confidence to the newsmen gathered around, awaiting the Secretary General's arrival, that their talks would bring an end to Katanga's violence.

Then came the explosive entry of an excited reporter who announced, "President Tshombe, Mr. Hammarskjöld is dead."

In New York City, this stunning news that the UN Secretary General had paid with his life while serving the world organization's peace efforts, came in a brief radio and television announcement at eight A.M. Thereafter, it was futile for anyone who cared about the end of this great statesman to get much from either radio or television. In short, things as usual, with no interruptions of news bulletins to disturb the regular programmed fare of soap opera serials, until much later in the afternoon and in the evening. It seemed unreal.

Delayed reaction and unreality indeed had permeated all the episodes leading up to and after the crash of the unescorted DC-6B, carrying Hammarskjöld and sixteen others, into flaming wreckage in the Congo bush. The rescue party, which had taken many many hours to get into action, had had to hack its way through the thick jungle to reach the scene of the tragedy. Later, autopsies of Hammarskjöld's unscorched body (he had been thrown clear of the flames) revealed he had not died instantly and might well have been saved had the rescue party arrived hours earlier.

There was only one survivor, and he was Harold M. Julian, a UN security guard. Although critically injured, he was able to state coherently that a series of explosions had rocked the aircraft and that he wasn't clear whether it had been engine trouble. Julian revealed that, just after landing clearance had been received from the Ndola tower, Hammarskjöld had ordered the pilot to remain airborne and to change course. Had the plane been attacked by one of Katanga's two jet fighters as later reported by witnesses of the fatal crash? Had there been sabotage? Had there been pilot error or mechanical failure? Might it have been cold-blooded murder?

Regrettably, from both a human and investigative standpoint, Harold Julian lived only a few days after his rescue and was unable, because of his lapsing strength, to supply detailed information.

"Who killed Dag Hammarskjöld?" quickly became an international parlor question, as a shocked world mourned and wondered who could possibly replace the overwhelmingly strong personality who had guided the UN through so many crises.

The magnificent UN Hammarskjöld Library stands in New York at the foot of 42nd Street as a daily reminder to the thousands who enter the building that there was a leader of this world body whom many worshipped to an extraordinary degree. These followers yet refuse to lower the curtain on the mysterious drama of his death.

When he died, Hammarskjöld had been working on a translation very dear to his heart—that of a work by the contemporary Jewish philosopher-mystic, Martin Buber, *I and Thou*. He had been completely imbued with the challenge of finding just the right linguistic form for what he termed "Buber's intensely beautiful, intensely personal and Old Testament prose." He had said the translation would be something of a personal declaration from him, too, because he found that Buber's ideas often corresponded to his own.

In our simplified portrait of Hammarskjöld, we finally come to the heart, soul and stamina of the slim, sandy-haired, gentle-looking Swede with the iron will and the brawn of the skilled mountaineer he was.

One cannot speak of the heart and soul of a man without speaking of his loves. If Dag Hammarskjöld disdained sexual love, he nevertheless was in love with two other entities, perhaps, to the philosopher, not so opposite as they seem. Dag was ardently in love with a bright sunny vital thing called Life. But spiritual bigamist that he was, he yielded with almost equal ardor to that dark and mysterious persuader, Death.

There isn't any doubt, from Hammarskjöld's writings, that death, so sure to come to him one day as to all others, held for him an uncommon fascination. One might say he was, in fact, often preoccupied with it; and he wrote about it repeatedly. Sometimes, he spoke of it detachedly; other times, during his many moods of premonition of death, he would see himself dead.

Detached, he wrote about it this way: "Your body must become familiar with its death, in all its possible forms and degrees, as a self evident, imminent, and emotionally neutral step on the way towards the goal you have found worthy of your life."

When he envisioned himself personally in the final entrapment, he put it this way in a poem which describes his death as a martyr's sacrifice:

> *I have watched the others:*
> *Now I am the victim,*
> *Strapped fast to the altar*
> *For sacrifice.*
> *Dumb, my naked body*
> *Endures the stoning, dumb*
> *When slit up and the live*
> *Heart is plucked out . . .*

In another mood, imagining himself in line for death, he tries to show resigned indifference:

> *What have I to fear?*
> *If their arrows hit,*
> *If their arrows kill,*
> *What is there in that to cry about?*
> *Others have gone before,*
> *Others will follow.*

It would be consoling to believe that Hammarskjöld, diplomat and poet of peace, has found in death what he once dreamed and penned in his diary in 1955:

"In a dream I walked with God through the deep places of creation; past walls that receded and gates that opened, through hall after hall of silence, darkness and refreshment—the dwelling place of souls acquainted with light and warmth—until, around me, was an infinity into which we all flowed together and lived anew, like the rings made by raindrops falling upon wide expanses of calm dark waters."

HEROES FOR OUR TIMES SURVEY

(Results of the poll conducted among members of the Overseas Press Club of America to determine who are the heroes for our times. The names are listed in order of the number of votes each received.)

Winston S. Churchill

Franklin D. Roosevelt

John F. Kennedy

Dr. Jonas Salk

Mahatma Gandhi

Eleanor Roosevelt

Pope John XXIII

Albert Schweitzer

Albert Einstein

Harry S Truman

Martin Luther King

Dag Hammarskjöld

Adlai E. Stevenson

Dwight D. Eisenhower

Douglas MacArthur

Helen Keller

George C. Marshall

Dr. Alexander Fleming

Carl Sandburg

Edward R. Murrow

Charles A. Lindbergh

Konrad Adenauer

J. Robert Oppenheimer

Pablo Casals

Walt Disney

Henry Ford

Moshe Dayan

David Ben-Gurion

Margaret Sanger

John Glenn

Bob Hope

Henry R. Luce

Billy Graham

Herbert Hoover

Norman Thomas

Ernest Hemingway

Pablo Picasso

David Sarnoff

Dr. Benjamin Spock

Charles De Gaulle

Dr. Tom Dooley

Lyndon B. Johnson

Roy Wilkins

Thomas Alva Edison

Robert Frost

J. Edgar Hoover

Marian Anderson

Bernard Baruch

Leonard Bernstein

Ralph Bunch

William F. Fulbright

Chief Albert John Luthuli

Arturo Toscanini

Woodrow Wilson

Jawaharlal Nehru

Fiorello H. La Guardia

Joe Louis

Bertrand Russell

George Herman ("Babe") Ruth

Dr. Albert Sabin

Rachel Carson

Thurgood Marshall

Boris Pasternak

Pope Paul VI

Norman Vincent Peale

Walter Reuther

Jackie Robinson

George Bernard Shaw

Orville and Wilbur Wright

Frank Lloyd Wright

Jane Addams

The Beatles

Mary McLeod Bethune

Pearl Buck

George Washington Carver

Dr. Michael E. De Bakey

Everett M. Dirksen

Enrico Fermi

Dr. Sigmund Freud

Averell Harriman

Helen Hayes

Robert F. Kennedy

Clare Boothe Luce

Mickey Mantle

Margaret Mead

John D. Rockefeller

Carlos P. Romulo

John Steinbeck

U Thant

Earl Warren

H. Rap Brown

Stokely Carmichael

James B. Conant

Marie Curie

John Foster Dulles

Robert H. Goddard

Arthur Goldberg

Roy Howard

Danny Kaye

Jacqueline Kennedy

John Maynard Keynes

Edward V. Rickenbacker

Theodore Roosevelt

Charles M. Schultz

Thomas Watson Jr.

HEROES FOR OUR TIMES

A Photographic Gallery
edited by Cornell Capa

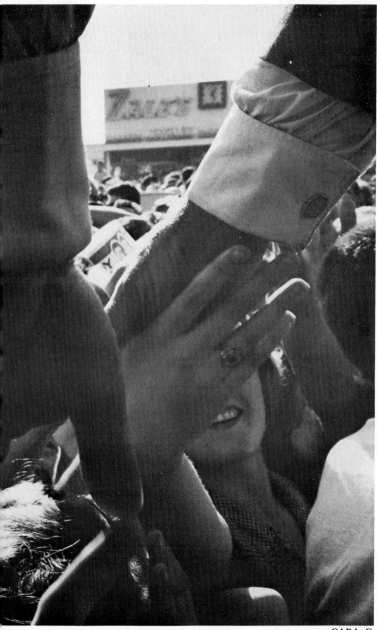

CAPA, C.

MARGARET BOURKE-WHITE has been a LIFE staff photographer since its first issue. A war-correspondent, a writer, a woman of indomitable courage, she was the last person to interview Ghandi, six hours before he was assassinated.

CORNELL CAPA's involvement in reporting politics in photographs began with Adlai Stevenson, a man he has deeply admired. He photographed John F. Kennedy's campaign and his "First Hundred Days" in Washington.

ROBERT CAPA, chronicler of five wars, died in 1954 covering one in Indochina. He left a legacy of photographs that indict war's inhumanity. The OPC-LIFE Annual Award given in his name reads: "For superlative photography, requiring exceptional courage and enterprise."

PHILIPPE HALSMAN is an outstanding photographer, author, teacher and lecturer of depth and wit. His portraits of Churchill, Einstein and Salk included in this gallery are a fair sampling of his brilliant work as a portraitist.

YOUSUF KARSH made the signature "Karsh of Ottawa" world famous. His distinctive style is instantly recognizable on all his portraits of celebrated contemporaries like those of Pope John, Mrs. Eleanor Roosevelt and Dag Hammarskjold included.

THOMAS D. McAVOY covered the Washington political world for LIFE from 1936 until 1949. One famous set of early candid pictures of President Roosevelt at his desk led to a White House ban on candid pictures of the President.

PAUL SCHUTZER's death in the Arab-Israel war in 1967 cut short his brilliant career. His youthful exuberance struck a tragic and sympathizing chord in life and death with his favored subjects, the Kennedys and Martin Luther King, Jr.

W. EUGENE SMITH, a giant of American photojournalism, is famous for his tensely moving and beautiful photographic essays which he pioneered and which were published in LIFE. The essay on Albert Schweitzer is especially memorable.

Acknowledgment is made to the overseas press club, photographer-members for their courtesy and cooperation and to LIFE Magazine for the photographs of Franklin D. Roosevelt, Mahatma Ghandi, and Martin Luther King, Jr.

CHURCHILL/HALSMAN

MRS. ROOSEVELT/KARSH

SCHWEITZER/SMITH

GHANDI/BOURKE-WHITE

SALK/HALSMAN

JOHN XXIII/KARSH

KING/SCHUTZER

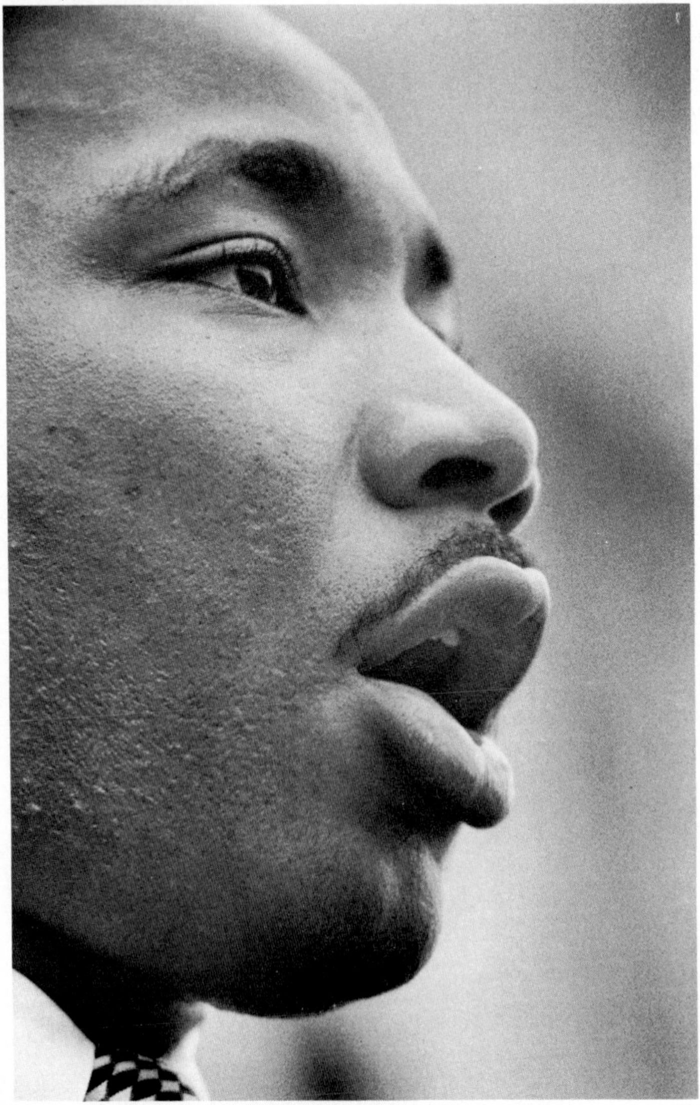

EINSTEIN/HALSMAN

TRUMAN/CAPA, R.